THE SCIENCE OF RIGHT

THE SCIENCE OF RIGHT

by Immanual Kant

translated by W. Hastie

Start Publishing PD LLC
Copyright © 2024 by Start Publishing PD LLC

All rights reserved, including the right to reproduce this book or portions thereof in any form whatsoever.

Start Publishing PD is a registered trademark of Start Publishing PD LLC
Manufactured in the United States of America

Cover art: Shutterstock/Taisiya Kozorez

Cover design: Jennifer Do

10 9 8 7 6 5 4 3 2 1

ISBN 979-8-8809-2039-6

INTRODUCTION

A. What the Science of Right is.

The Science of Right has for its object the principles of all the laws which it is possible to promulgate by external legislation. Where there is such a legislation, it becomes, in actual application to it, a system of positive right and law; and he who is versed in the knowledge of this system is called a jurist or jurisconsult (jurisconsultus). A practical jurisconsult (jurisperitus), or a professional lawyer, is one who is skilled in the knowledge of positive external laws, and who can apply them to cases that may occur in experience. Such practical knowledge of positive right, and law, may be regarded as belonging to jurisprudence (jurisprudentia) in the original sense of the term. But the theoretical knowledge of right and law in principle, as distinguished from positive laws and empirical cases, belongs to the pure science of right (jurisscientia). The science of right thus designates the philosophical and systematic knowledge of the principles of natural right. And it is from this science that the immutable principles of all positive legislation must be derived by practical jurists and lawgivers.

B. What is Right?

This question may be said to be about as embarrassing to the jurist as the well-known question, "What is truth?" is to the logician. It is all the more so, if, on reflection, he strives to avoid tautology in his reply and recognise the fact that a reference to what holds true merely of the laws of some one country at a particular time is not a solution of the general problem thus proposed. It is quite easy to state what may be right in particular cases (quid sit juris), as being what the laws of a certain place and of a certain time say or may have said; but it is much more difficult to determine whether what they have enacted is right in itself, and to lay down a universal criterion by which right and wrong in general, and what is just and unjust, may be recognised. All this may remain entirely hidden even from the practical jurist until he abandon his empirical principles for a time and search in the pure reason for the sources of such judgements, in order to lay a real foundation for actual positive legislation. In this search, his empirical laws may, indeed, furnish him with excellent guidance; but a merely empirical system that is void of rational principles is, like the wooden head in the fable of Phaedrus, fine enough in appearance, but unfortunately it wants brain.

1. The conception of right- as referring to a corresponding obligation which is

the moral aspect of it- in the first place, has regard only to the external and practical relation of one person to another, in so far as they can have influence upon each other, immediately or mediately, by their actions as facts. 2. In the second place, the conception of right does not indicate the relation of the action of an individual to the wish or the mere desire of another, as in acts of benevolence or of unkindness, but only the relation of his free action to the freedom of action of the other. 3. And, in the third place, in this reciprocal relation of voluntary actions, the conception of right does not take into consideration the matter of the matter of the act of will in so far as the end which any one may have in view in willing it is concerned. In other words, it is not asked in a question of right whether any one on buying goods for his own business realizes a profit by the transaction or not; but only the form of the transaction is taken into account, in considering the relation of the mutual acts of will. Acts of will or voluntary choice are thus regarded only in so far as they are free, and as to whether the action of one can harmonize with the freedom of another, according to a universal law.

Right, therefore, comprehends the whole of the conditions under which the voluntary actions of any one person can be harmonized in reality with the voluntary actions of every other person, according to a universal law of freedom.

C. Universal Principle of Right.

"Every action is right which in itself, or in the maxim on which it proceeds, is such that it can coexist along with the freedom of the will of each and all in action, according to a universal law."

If, then, my action or my condition generally can coexist with the freedom of every other, according to a universal law, any one does me a wrong who hinders me in the performance of this action, or in the maintenance of this condition. For such a hindrance or obstruction cannot coexist with freedom according to universal laws.

It follows also that it cannot be demanded as a matter of right, that this universal principle of all maxims shall itself be adopted as my maxim, that is, that I shall make it the maxim of my actions. For any one may be free, although his freedom is entirely indifferent to me, or even if I wished in my heart to infringe it, so long as I do not actually violate that freedom by my external action. Ethics, however, as distinguished from jurisprudence, imposes upon me the obligation to make the fulfillment of right a maxim of my conduct.

The universal law of right may then be expressed thus: "Act externally in such a manner that the free exercise of thy will may be able to coexist with the freedom of all others, according to a universal law." This is undoubtedly a law which imposes obligation upon me; but it does not at all imply and still less command that I ought, merely on account of this obligation, to limit my freedom to these very conditions. Reason in this connection says only that it is restricted thus far by its idea, and may be likewise thus limited in fact by others; and it lays this down as a postulate which is not capable of further proof. As the object in view is not to teach virtue, but to explain what right is, thus far the law of right, as thus laid down, may not and should not be represented as a motive-principle of action.

D. Right is Conjoined with the Title or Authority to Compel.

The resistance which is opposed to any hindrance of an effect is in reality a furtherance of this effect and is in accordance with its accomplishment. Now, everything that is wrong is a hindrance of freedom, according to universal laws; and compulsion or constraint of any kind is a hindrance or resistance made to freedom. Consequently, if a certain exercise of freedom is itself a hindrance of the freedom that is according to universal laws, it is wrong; and the compulsion of constraint which is opposed to it is right, as being a hindering of a hindrance of freedom, and as being in accord with the freedom which exists in accordance with universal laws. Hence, according to the logical principle of contradiction, all right is accompanied with an implied title or warrant to bring compulsion to bear on any one who may violate it in fact.

E. Strict Right may be also Represented as the Possibility
of a Universal Reciprocal Compulsion in harmony with
the Freedom of All according to Universal Laws.

This proposition means the right is not to be regarded as composed of two different elements- obligation according to a law, and a title on the part of one who has bound another by his own free choice to compel him to perform. But it imports that the conception of right may be viewed as consisting immediately in the possibility of a universal reciprocal compulsion, in harmony with the freedom of all. As right in general has for its object only what is external in actions, strict right, as that with which nothing ethical is intermingled, requires no other motives of action than those that are merely external; for it is then pure right and is unmixed with any prescriptions of virtue. A strict right, then, in the exact sense of the term, is that which alone can be called wholly external. Now such right is founded, no doubt, upon the consciousness of the obligation of every individual according to the law; but if it is to be pure as such, it neither may nor should refer to this consciousness as a motive by which to determine the free act of the will. For this purpose, however, it founds upon the principle of the possibility of an external compulsion, such as may coexist with the freedom of every one according to universal laws. Accordingly, then, where it is said that a creditor has a right to demand from a debtor the payment of his debt, this does not mean merely that he can bring him to feel in his mind that reason obliges him to do this; but it means that he can apply an external compulsion to force any such one so to pay, and that this compulsion is quite consistent with the freedom of all, including the parties in question, according to a

THE SCIENCE OF RIGHT 7

universal law. Right and the title to compel, thus indicate the same thing.

The law of right, as thus enunciated, is represented as a reciprocal compulsion necessarily in accordance with the freedom of every one, under the principle of a universal freedom. It is thus, as it were, a representative construction of the conception of right, by exhibiting it in a pure intuitive perception a priori, after the analogy of the possibility of the free motions of bodies under the physical law of the equality of action and reaction. Now, as in pure mathematics, we cannot deduce the properties of its objects immediately from a mere abstract conception, but can only discover them by figurative construction or representation of its conceptions; so it is in like manner with the principle of right. It is not so much the mere formal conception of right, but rather that of a universal and equal reciprocal compulsion as harmonizing with it, and reduced under general laws, that makes representation of that conception possible. But just as those conceptions presented in dynamics are founded upon a merely formal representation of pure mathematics as presented in geometry, reason has taken care also to provide the understanding as far as possible with intuitive presentations a priori in behoof of a construction of the conception of right. The right in geometrical lines (rectum) is opposed, as the straight, to that which is curved and to that which is oblique. In the first opposition, there is involved an inner quality of the lines of such a nature that there is only one straight or right line possible between two given points. In the second case, again, the positions of two intersecting or meeting lines are of such a nature that there can likewise be only one line called the perpendicular, which is not more inclined to the one side than the other, and it divides space on either side into two equal parts. After the manner of this analogy, the science of right aims at determining what every one shall have as his own with mathematical exactness; but this is not to be expected in the ethical science of virtue, as it cannot but allow a certain latitude for exceptions. But, without passing into the sphere of ethics, there are two cases- known as the equivocal right of equity and necessity- which claim a juridical decision, yet for which no one can be found to give such a decision, and which, as regards their relation to rights, belong, as it were, to the "Intermundia" of Epicurus. These we must at the outset take apart from the special exposition of the science of right, to which we are now about to advance; and we may consider them now by way of supplement to these introductory explanations, in order that their uncertain conditions may not exert a disturbing influence on the fixed principles of the proper doctrine of right.

F. Supplementary Remarks on Equivocal Right.

(Jus Aequivocum).

With every right, in the strict acceptation (jus strictum), there is conjoined a right to compel. But it is possible to think of other rights of a wider kind (jus latum) in which the title to compel cannot be determined by any law. Now there are two real or supposed rights of this kind- equity and the right of necessity. The first alleges a right that is without compulsion; the second adopts a compulsion that is without right. This equivocalness, however, can be easily shown to rest on the peculiar fact that there are cases of doubtful right, for the decision of which no judge can be appointed.

I. Equity.

Equity (aequitas), regarded objectively, does not properly constitute a claim upon the moral duty of benevolence or beneficence on the part of others; but whoever insists upon anything on the ground of equity, founds upon his right to the same. In this case, however, the conditions are awanting that are requisite for the function of a judge in order that be might determine what or what kind of satisfaction can be done to this claim. When one of the partners of a mercantile company, formed under the condition of equal profits, has, however, done more than the other members, and in consequence has also lost more, it is in accordance with equity that he should demand from the company more than merely an equal share of advantage with the rest. But, in relation to strict right- if we think of a judge considering his case- he can furnish no definite data to establish how much more belongs to him by the contract; and in case of an action at law, such a demand would be rejected. A domestic servant, again, who might be paid his wages due to the end of his year of service in a coinage that became depreciated within that period, so that it would not be of the same value to him as it was when he entered on his engagement, cannot claim by right to be kept from loss on account of the unequal value of the money if he receives the due amount of it. He can only make an appeal on the ground of equity,- a dumb goddess who cannot claim a bearing of right,- because there was nothing bearing on this point in the contract of service, and a judge cannot give a decree on the basis of vague or indefinite conditions.

Hence it follows, that a court of equity, for the decision of disputed questions of right, would involve a contradiction. It is only where his own proper rights are concerned, and in matters in which he can decide, that a judge may or ought to give a hearing to equity. Thus, if the Crown is supplicated to give an indemnity to certain persons for loss or injury sustained in its service, it may undertake the burden of doing so, although, according to strict right, the claim might be rejected on the ground of the pretext that the parties in question undertook the performance of the service occasioning the loss, at their own risk.

The dictum of equity may be put thus: "The strictest right is the greatest wrong" (summum jus summa injuria). But this evil cannot be obviated by the forms of right, although it relates to a matter of right; for the grievance that it gives rise to can only be put before a "court of conscience" (forum poli), whereas every question of right must be taken before a civil court (forum soli).

II. The Right of Necessity.

The so-called right of necessity (jus necessitatis) is the supposed right or title, in case of the danger of losing my own life, to take away the life of another who has, in fact, done me no harm. It is evident that, viewed as a doctrine of right, this must involve a contradiction, For this is not the case of a wrongful aggressor making an unjust assault upon my life, and whom I anticipate by depriving him of his own (jus inculpatae tutelae); nor consequently is it a question merely of the recommendation of moderation which belongs to ethics as the doctrine of virtue, and not to jurisprudence as the doctrine of right. It is a question of the allowableness of using violence against one who has used none against me.

It is clear that the assertion of such a right is not to be understood objectively as being in accordance with what a law would prescribe, but merely subjectively, as proceeding on the assumption of how a sentence would be pronounced by a court in the case. There can, in fact, be no criminal law assigning the penalty of death to a man who, when shipwrecked and struggling in extreme danger for his life, and in order to save it, may thrust another from a plank on which he had saved himself. For the punishment threatened by the law could not possibly have greater power than the fear of the loss of life in the case in question. Such a penal law would thus fail altogether to exercise its intended effect; for the threat of an evil which is still uncertain- such as death by a judicial sentence- could not overcome the fear of an evil which is certain, as drowning is in such circumstances. An act of violent self-preservation, then, ought not to be considered as altogether beyond condemnation (inculpabile); it is only to be adjudged as exempt from punishment (impunibile). Yet this subjective condition of impunity, by a strange confusion of ideas, has been regarded by jurists as equivalent to objective lawfulness.

The dictum of the right of necessity is put in these terms: "Necessity has no law" (Necessitas non habet legem). And yet there cannot be a necessity that could make what is wrong lawful.

It is apparent, then, that in judgements relating both to "equity" and "the right of necessity," the equivocations involved arise from an interchange of the objective and subjective grounds that enter into the application of the principles of right, when viewed respectively by reason or by a judicial tribunal. What one may have good grounds for recognising as right, in itself, may not find confirmation in a court of justice; and what he must consider to be wrong, in itself, may obtain recognition in such a court. And the reason of this is that the conception of right is not taken in the two cases in one and the same sense.

DIVISION OF THE SCIENCE OF RIGHT.

A. General Division of the Duties of Right.

(Juridical Duties).

In this division we may very conveniently follow Ulpian, if his three formulae are taken in a general sense, which may not have been quite clearly in his mind, but which they are capable of being developed into or of receiving. They are the following:

1. Honeste vive. "Live rightly." juridical rectitude, or honour (honestas juridica), consists in maintaining one's own worth as a man in relation to others. This duty may be rendered by the proposition: "Do not make thyself a mere means for the use of others, but be to them likewise an end." This duty will be explained in the next formula as an obligation arising out of the right of humanity in our own person (lex justi).

2. Neminem laede. "Do wrong to no one." This formula may be rendered so as to mean: "Do no wrong to any one, even if thou shouldst be under the necessity, in observing this duty, to cease from all connection with others and to avoid all society" (lex juridica).

3. Suum cuique tribue. "Assign to every one what is his own." This may be rendered, "Enter, if wrong cannot be avoided, into a society with others in which every one may have secured to him what is his own." If this formula were to be simply translated, "Give every one his own," it would express an absurdity, for we cannot give any one what he already has. If it is to have a definite meaning, it must therefore run thus: "Enter into a state in which every one can have what is his own secured against the action of every other" (lex justitiae).

These three classical formulae, at the same time, represent principles which suggest a division of the system of juridical duties into internal duties, external duties, and those connecting duties which contain the latter as deduced from the principle of the former by subsumption.

B. Universal Division of Rights.

I. Natural Right and Positive Right. The system of rights, viewed as a scientific system of doctrines, is divided into natural right and positive right. Natural right rests upon pure rational principles a priori; positive or statutory right is what proceeds from the will of a legislator.

II. Innate Right and Acquired Right. The system of rights may again be regarded in reference to the implied powers of dealing morally with others as bound by obligations, that is, as furnishing a legal title of action in relation to them. Thus viewed, the system is divided into innate right and acquired right. Innate right is that right which belongs to every one by nature, independent of all juridical acts of experience. Acquired right is that right which is founded upon such juridical acts.

Innate right may also be called the "internal mine and thine" (meum vel tuum internum) for external right must always be acquired.

There is only one Innate Right, the Birthright of Freedom.

Freedom is independence of the compulsory will of another; and in so far as it can coexist with the freedom of all according to a universal law, it is the one sole original, inborn right belonging to every man in virtue of his humanity. There is, indeed, an innate equality belonging to every man which consists in his right to be independent of being bound by others to anything more than that to which he may also reciprocally bind them. It is, consequently, the inborn quality of every man in virtue of which he ought to be his own master by right (sui juris). There is, also, the natural quality of justness attributable to a man as naturally of unimpeachable right (justi), because be has done no wrong to any one prior to his own juridical actions. And, further, there is also the innate right of common action on the part of every man, so that he may do towards others what does not infringe their rights or take away anything that is theirs unless they are willing to appropriate it; such merely to communicate thought, to narrate anything, or to promise something whether truly and honestly, or untruly and dishonestly (veriloquim aut falsiloquim), for it rests entirely upon these others whether they will believe or trust in it or not.* But all these rights or titles are already included in the principle of innate freedom, and are not really distinguished from it, even as dividing members under a higher species of right.

*It is customary to designate every untruth that is spoken intentionally as such, although it may be in a frivolous manner a lie, or falsehood (mendacium), because it may do harm, at least in so far as any one who repeats it in good faith may be made a laughing-stock of to others on account of his easy credulity. But in the juridical sense, only that untruth is called a lie which immediately infringes the right of another, such as a false allegation of a contract having been concluded, when the allegation is put forward in order to deprive some one of what is his (falsiloquim dolosum). This distinction of conceptions so closely allied is not without foundation; because on the occasion of a simple statement of one's thoughts, it is always free for another to take them as he may; and yet the resulting repute, that such a one is a man whose word cannot be trusted, comes so close to the opprobrium of directly calling him a liar, that the boundary-line separating what, in such a case, belongs to jurisprudence, and what is special to ethics, can hardly be otherwise drawn.

The reason why such a division into separate rights has been introduced into the system of natural right, viewed as including all that is innate, was not without a purpose. Its object was to enable proof to be more readily put forward in case of any controversy arising about an acquired right, and questions emerging either with reference to a fact that might be in doubt, or, if that were established, in reference to a right under dispute. For the party repudiating an obligation, and on whom the burden of proof (onus probandi) might be incumbent, could thus methodically refer to his innate right of freedom as specified under various relations in detail, and could therefore found upon them equally as different titles of right.

In the relation of innate right, and consequently of the internal mine and thine, there is therefore not rights, but only one right. And, accordingly, this highest division of rights into innate and acquired, which evidently consists of two members extremely unequal in their contents is properly placed in the introduction; and the subdivisions of the science of right may be referred in detail to the external mine and thine.

C. Methodical Division of the Science of Right.

The highest division of the system of natural right should not be- as it is frequently put- into "natural right" and "social right," but into natural right and civil right. The first constitutes private right; the second, public right. For it is not the "social state" but the "civil state" that is opposed to the "state of nature"; for in the "state of nature" there may well be society of some kind, but there is no "civil" society, as an institution securing the mine and thine by public laws. It is thus that right, viewed under reference to the state of nature, is specially called private right. The whole of the principles of right will therefore fall to be expounded under the two subdivisions of private right and public right.

FIRST PART. PRIVATE RIGHT.
The System of those Laws Which Require No External Promulgation.
CHAPTER I. Of the Mode of Having Anything External as One's Own.
1. The Meaning of "Mine" in Right
(Meum Juris).

Anything is "Mine" by right, or is rightfully mine, when I am so connected with it, that if any other person should make use of it without my consent, he would do me a lesion or injury. The subjective condition of the use of anything is possession of it.

An external thing, however as such could only be mine, if I may assume it to be possible that I can be wronged by the use which another might make of it when it is not actually in my possession. Hence it would be a contradiction to have anything external as one's own, were not the conception of possession capable of two different meanings, as sensible possession that is perceivable by the senses, and rational possession that is perceivable only by the intellect. By the former is to be understood a physical possession, and by the latter, a purely juridical possession of the same object.

The description of an object as "external to me" may signify either that it is merely "different and distinct from me as a subject," or that it is also "a thing placed outside of me, and to be found elsewhere in space or time." Taken in the first sense, the term possession signifies rational possession; and, in the second sense, it must mean empirical possession. A rational or intelligible possession, if such be possible, is possession viewed apart from physical holding or detention (detentio).

2. Juridical Postulate of the Practical Reason.

It is possible to have any external object of my will as mine. In other words, a maxim to this effect- were it to become law- that any object on which the will can be exerted must remain objectively in itself without an owner, as res nullius, is contrary to the principle of right.

For an object of any act of my will, is something that it would be physically within my power to use. Now, suppose there were things that by right should absolutely not be in our power, or, in other words, that it would be wrong or inconsistent with the freedom of all, according to universal law, to make use of them. On this supposition, freedom would so far be depriving itself of the use of its voluntary activity, in thus putting useable objects out of all possibility of use. In practical relations, this would be to annihilate them, by making them res nullius, notwithstanding the fact act acts of will in relation to such things would formally harmonize, in the actual use of them, with the external freedom of all according to universal laws. Now the pure practical reason lays down only formal laws as principles to regulate the exercise of the will; and therefore abstracts from the matter of the act of will, as regards the other qualities of the object, which is considered only in so far as it is an object of the activity of the will. Hence the practical reason cannot contain, in reference to such an object, an absolute prohibition of its use, because this would involve a contradiction of external freedom with itself. An object of my free will, however, is one which I have the physical capability of making some use of at will, since its use stands in my power (in potentia). This is to be distinguished from having the object brought under my disposal (in postestatem meam reductum), which supposes not a capability merely, but also a particular act of the free-will. But in order to consider something merely as an object of my will as such, it is sufficient to be conscious that I have it in my power. It is therefore an assumption a priori of the practical reason to regard and treat every object within the range of my free exercise of will as objectively a possible mine or thine.

This postulate may be called "a permissive law" of the practical reason, as giving us a special title which we could not evolve out of the mere conceptions of right generally. And this title constitutes the right to impose upon all others an obligation, not otherwise laid upon them, to abstain from the use of certain objects of our free choice, because we have already taken them into our possession. Reason wills that this shall be recognised as a valid principle, and it does so as practical reason; and it is enabled by means of this postulate a priori to enlarge its range of activity in practice.

3. Possession and Ownership.

Any one who would assert the right to a thing as his must be in possession of it as an object. Were he not its actual possessor or owner, he could not be wronged or injured by the use which another might make of it without his consent. For, should anything external to him, and in no way connected with him by right, affect this object, it could not affect himself as a subject, nor do him any wrong, unless he stood in a relation of ownership to it.

4. Exposition of the Conception of the.

External Mine and Thine.

There can only be three external objects of my will in the activity of choice:

(1) A corporeal thing external to me;

(2) The free-will of another in the performance of a particular act (praestatio);

(3) The state of another in relation to myself.

These correspond to the categories of substance, causality, and reciprocity; and they form the practical relations between me and external objects, according to the laws of freedom.

A. I can only call a corporeal thing or an object in space "mine," when, even although not in physical possession of it, I am able to assert that I am in possession of it in another real nonphysical sense. Thus, I am not entitled to call an apple mine merely because I hold it in my hand or possess it physically; but only when I am entitled to say, "I possess it, although I have laid it out of my hand, and wherever it may lie." In like manner, I am not entitled to say of the ground, on which I may have laid myself down, that therefore it is mine; but only when I can rightly assert that it still remains in my possession, although I may have left the spot. For any one who, in the former appearances of empirical possession, might wrench the apple out of my hand, or drag me away from my resting-place, would, indeed, injure me in respect of the inner "mine" of freedom, but not in respect of the external "mine," unless I could assert that I was in the possession of the object, even when not actually holding it physically. And if I could not do this, neither could I call the apple or the spot mine.

B. I cannot call the performance of something by the action of the will of another "mine," if I can only say "it has come into my possession at the same time with a promise" (pactum re initum); but only if I am able to assert "I am in possession of the will of the other, so as to determine him to the performance of a particular act, although the time for the performance of it has not yet come." In the latter case, the promise belongs to the nature of things actually held as possessed, and as an active obligation I can reckon it mine; and this holds good not only if I have the thing promised- as in the first case- already in my possession, but even although I do not yet possess it in fact. Hence, I must be able to regard myself in thought as independent of that empirical form of possession that is limited by the condition of time and as being, nevertheless, in possession of the object.

C. I cannot call a wife, a child, a domestic, or, generally, any other person "mine" merely because I command them at present as belonging to my household, or because I have them under control, and in my power and possession. But I can call them mine, if, although they may have withdrawn themselves from my control and I do not therefore possess them empirically, I can still say "I possess them by my mere will, provided they exist anywhere in space or time; and, consequently, my possession of them is purely juridical." They belong, in fact, to my possessions, only when and so far as I can assert this as a matter of right.

5. Definition of the Conception of the
External Mine and Thine.

Definitions are nominal or real. A nominal definition is sufficient merely to distinguish the object defined from all other objects, and it springs out of a complete and definite exposition of its conception. A real definition further suffices for a deduction of the conception defined, so as to furnish a knowledge of the reality of the object. The nominal definition of the external "mine" would thus be: "The external mine is anything outside of myself, such that any hindrance of my use of it at will would be doing me an injury or wrong as an infringement of that freedom of mine which may coexist with the freedom of all others according to a universal law." The real definition of this conception may be put thus: "The external mine is anything outside of myself, such that any prevention of my use of it would be a wrong, although I may not be in possession of it so as to be actually holding it as an object." I must be in some kind of possession of an external object, if the object is to be regarded as mine; for, otherwise, anyone interfering with this object would not, in doing so, affect me; nor, consequently, would he thereby do me any wrong. Hence, according to SS 4, a rational possession (possessio noumenon) must be assumed as possible, if there is to be rightly an external mine and thine. Empirical possession is thus only phenomenal possession or holding (detention) of the object in the sphere of sensible appearance (possessio phenomenon), although the object which I possess is not regarded in this practical relation as itself a phenomenon- according to the exposition of the Transcendental Analytic in the Critique of Pure Reason- but as a thing in itself. For in the Critique of Pure Reason the interest of reason turns upon the theoretical knowledge of the nature of things and how far reason can go in such knowledge. But here reason has to deal with the practical determination of the action of the will according to laws of freedom, whether the object is perceivable through the senses or merely thinkable by the pure understanding. And right, as under consideration, is a pure practical conception of the reason in relation to the exercise of the will under laws of freedom.

And, hence, it is not quite correct to speak of "possessing" a right to this or that object, but it should rather be said that an object is possessed in a purely juridical way; for a right is itself the rational possession of an object, and to "possess a possession," would be an expression without meaning.

6. Deduction of the Conception of a Purely Juridical
Possession of an External Object (Possessio Noumenon).

The question, "How is an external mine and thine possible?" resolves itself into this other question: "How is a merely juridical or rational possession possible?" And this second question resolves itself again into a third: "How is a synthetic proposition in right possible a priori?"

All propositions of right- as juridical propositions- are propositions a priori, for they are practical laws of reason (dictamina rationis). But the juridical proposition a priori respecting empirical possession is analytical; for it says nothing more than what follows by the principle of contradiction, from the conception of such possession; namely, that if I am the holder of a thing in the way of being physically connected with it, any one interfering with it without my consent- as, for instance, in wrenching an apple out of my hand- affects and detracts from my freedom as that which is internally mine; and consequently the maxim of his action is in direct contradiction to the axiom of right. The proposition expressing the principle of an empirical rightful possession does not therefore go beyond the right of a person in reference to himself.

On the other hand, the proposition expressing the possibility of the possession of a thing external to me, after abstraction of all the conditions of empirical possession in space and time- consequently presenting the assumption of the possibility of a possessio noumenon- goes beyond these limiting conditions; and because this proposition asserts a possession even without physical holding, as necessary to the conception of the external mine and thine, it is synthetical. And thus it becomes a problem for reason to show how such a proposition, extending its range beyond the conception of empirical possession, is possible a priori.

In this manner, for instance, the act of taking possession of a particular portion of the soil is a mode exercising the private free-will without being an act of usurpation. The possessor founds upon the innate right of common possession of the surface of the earth, and upon the universal will corresponding a priori to it, which allows a private possession of the soil; because what are mere things would be otherwise made in themselves and by a law into unappropriable objects. Thus a first appropriator acquires originally by primary possession a particular portion of the ground; and by right (jure) he resists every other person who would hinder him in the private use of it, although, while the "state of nature" continues, this cannot be done by juridical means (de jure), because a public law does not yet exist.

And although a piece of ground should be regarded as free, or declared to be such, so as to be for the public use of all without distinction, yet it cannot be said that it is thus free by nature and originally so, prior to any juridical act. For there would be a real relation already incorporated in such a piece of ground by the very fact that the possession of it was denied to any particular individual; and as this public freedom of the ground would be a prohibition of it to every particular individual, this presupposes a common possession of it which cannot take effect without a contract. A piece of ground, however, which can only become publicly free by contract, must actually be in the possession of all those associated together, who mutually interdict or suspend each other, from any particular or private use of it.

This original community of the soil and of the things upon it (communio fundi originaria), is an idea which has objective and practical juridical reality and is entirely different from the idea of a primitive community of things, which is a fiction. For the latter would have had to be founded as a form of society, and must have taken its rise from a contract by which all renounced the right of private possession, so that by uniting the property owned by each into a whole, it was thus transformed into a common possession. But had such an event taken place, history must have presented some evidence of it. To regard such a procedure as the original mode of taking possession, and to hold that the particular possessions of every individual may and ought to be grounded upon it, is evidently a contradiction.

Possession (possessio) is to be distinguished from habitation as mere residence (sedes); and the act of taking possession of the soil in the intention of acquiring it once for all, is also to be distinguished from settlement or domicile (incolatus), which is a continuous private possession of a place that is dependent on the presence of the individual upon it. We have not here to deal with the question of domiciliary settlement, as that is a secondary juridical act which may follow upon possession, or may not occur at all; for as such it could not involve an original possession, but only a secondary possession derived from the consent of others.

Simple physical possession, or holding of the soil, involves already certain relations of right to the thing, although it is certainly not sufficient to enable me to regard it as mine. Relative to others, so far as they know, it appears as a first possession in harmony with the law of external freedom; and, at the same time, it is embraced in the universal original possession which contains a priori the fundamental principle of the possibility of a private possession. Hence to disturb the first occupier or holder of a portion of the soil in his use of it is a lesion or wrong done to him. The first taking of possession has therefore a title of right (titulus possessionis) in its favour, which is simply the principle of the original common possession; and the saying that "It is well for those who are in possession" (beati possidentes), when one is not bound to authenticate his possession, is a principle of natural right that establishes the juridical act of taking possession, as a ground of acquisition upon which every first possessor may found.

It has been shown in the Critique of Pure Reason that in theoretical principles a priori, an intuitional perception a priori must be supplied in connection with any given conception; and, consequently, were it a question of a purely theoretical principle, something would have to be added to the conception of the possession of an object to make it real. But in respect of the practical principle under consideration, the procedure is just the converse of the theoretical process; so that all the conditions of perception which form the foundation of empirical possession must be abstracted or taken away in order to extend the range of the juridical conception beyond the empirical sphere, and in order to be able to apply the postulate, that every external object of the free activity of my will, so far as I have it in my power, although not in the possession of it, may be reckoned as juridically mine.

The possibility of such a possession, with consequent deduction of the conception of a nonempirical possession, is founded upon the juridical postulate of the practical reason, that "It is a juridical duty so to act towards others that what is external and useable may come into the possession or become the property of some one." And this postulate is conjoined with the exposition of the conception that what is externally one's own is founded upon a possession, that is not physical. The possibility of such a possession, thus conceived, cannot, however, be proved or comprehended in itself, because it is a rational conception for which no empirical perception can be furnished; but it follows as an immediate consequence from the postulate that has been enunciated. For, if it is necessary to act according to that juridical principle, the rational or intelligible condition of a purely juridical possession must also be possible. It need astonish no one, then, that the theoretical aspect of the principles of the external mine and thine is lost from view in the rational sphere of pure intelligence and presents no extension of knowledge; for the conception of freedom upon which they rest does not admit of any theoretical deduction of its possibility, and it can only be inferred from the practical law of reason, called the categorical imperative, viewed as a fact.

7. Application of the Principle of the Possibility of
an External Mine and Thine to Objects of Experience.

The conception of a purely juridical possession is not an empirical conception dependent on conditions of space and time, and yet it has practical reality. As such it must be applicable to objects of experience, the knowledge of which is independent of the conditions of space and time. The rational process by which the conception of right is brought into relation to such objects so as to constitute a possible external mine and thine, is as follows. The conception of right, being contained merely in reason, cannot be immediately applied to objects of experience, so as to give the conception of an empirical possession, but must be applied directly to the mediating conception, in the understanding, of possession in general; so that, instead of physical holding (detentio) as an empirical representation of possession, the formal conception or thought of having, abstracted from all conditions of space and time, is conceived by the mind, and only as implying that an object is in my power and at my disposal (in potestate mea positum esse). In this relation, the term external does not signify existence in another place than where I am, nor my resolution and acceptance at another time than the moment in which I have the offer of a thing: it signifies only an object different from or other than myself. Now the practical reason by its law of right wills, that I shall think the mine and thine in application to objects, not according to sensible conditions, but apart from these and from the possession they indicate; because they refer to determinations of the activity of the will that are in accordance with the laws of freedom. For it is only a conception of the understanding that can be brought under the rational conception of right. I may therefore say that I possess a field, although it is in quite a different place from that on which I actually find myself. For the question here is not concerning an intellectual relation to the object, but I have the thing practically in my power and at my disposal, which is a conception of possession realized by the understanding and independent of relations of space; and it is mine, because my will, in determining itself to any particular use of it, is not in conflict with the law of external freedom. Now it is just in abstraction from physical possession of the object of my free-will in the sphere of sense, that the practical reason wills that a rational possession of it shall be thought, according to intellectual conceptions which are not empirical, but contain a priori the conditions of rational possession. Hence it is in this fact, that we found the ground of the validity of such a rational conception of possession possessio noumenon) as a principle of a universally valid legislation. For such a legislation is implied and contained in the expression, "This external object is mine," because an obligation is thereby imposed upon all others in respect of it, who would otherwise not have been obliged to abstain from the use of this object.

The mode, then, of having something external to myself as mine, consists in a specially juridical connection of the will of the subject with that object, independently of the empirical relations to it in space and in time, and in accordance with the conception of a rational possession. A particular spot on the earth is not externally mine because I occupy it with my body; for the question here discussed refers only to my external freedom, and consequently it affects only the possession of myself, which is not a thing external to me, and therefore only involves an internal right. But if I continue to be in possession of the spot, although I have taken myself away from it and gone to another place, only under that condition is my external right concerned in connection with it. And to make the continuous possession of this spot by my person a condition of having it as mine, must either be to assert that it is not possible at all to have anything external as one's own, which is contrary to the postulate in SS 2, or to require, in order that this external possession may be possible, that I shall be in two places at the same time. But this amounts to saying that I must be in a place and also not in it, which is contradictory and absurd.

This position may be applied to the case in which I have accepted a promise; for my having and possession in respect of what has been promised become established on the ground of external right. This right is not to be annulled by the fact that the promiser having said at one time, "This thing shall be yours," again at a subsequent time says, "My will now is that the thing shall not be yours." In such relations of rational right, the conditions hold just the same as if the promiser had, without any interval of time between them, made the two declarations of his will, "This shall be yours," and also "This shall not be yours"; which manifestly contradicts itself.

The same thing holds, in like manner, of the conception of the juridical possession of a person as belonging to the Having of a subject, whether it be a wife, a child, or a servant. The relations of right involved in a household, and the reciprocal possession of all its members, are not annulled by the capability of separating from each other in space; because it is by juridical relations that they are connected, and the external mine and thine, as in the former cases, rests entirely upon the assumption of the possibility of a purely rational possession, without the accompaniment of physical detention or holding of the object.

Reason is forced to a critique of its juridically practical function in special reference to the conception of the external mine and thine, by the antinomy of the propositions enunciated regarding the possibility of such a form of possession. For these give rise to an inevitable dialectic, in which a thesis and an antithesis set up equal claims to the validity of two conflicting conditions. Reason is thus compelled, in its practical function in relation to right- as it was in its theoretical function- to make a distinction between possession as a phenomenal appearance presented to the senses, and that possession which is rational and thinkable only by the understanding.

Thesis.- The thesis, in this case, is: "It is possible to have something external as mine, although I am not in possession of it."

Antithesis.- The antithesis is: "It is not possible to have anything external as mine, if I am not in possession of it."

Solution.- The solution is: "Both Propositions are true"; the former when I mean empirical possession (possessio phaenomenon), the latter when I understand by the same term, a purely rational possession (possessio noumenon).

But the possibility of a rational possession, and consequently of an external mine and thine, cannot be comprehended by direct insight, but must be deduced from the practical reason. And in this relation it is specially noteworthy that the practical reason without intuitional perceptions, and even without requiring such an element a priori, can extend its range by the mere elimination of empirical conditions, as justified by the law of freedom, and can thus establish synthetical propositions a priori. The proof of this in the practical connection, as will be shown afterwards, can be adduced in an analytical manner.

8. To Have Anything External as One's Own is only Possible in a Juridical or Civil State of Society under the Regulation of a Public Legislative Power.

If, by word or deed, I declare my will that some external thing shall be mine, I make a declaration that every other person is obliged to abstain from the use of this object of my exercise of will; and this imposes an obligation which no one would be under, without such a juridical act on my part. But the assumption of this act at the same time involves the admission that I am obliged reciprocally to observe a similar abstention towards every other in respect of what is externally theirs; for the obligation in question arises from a universal rule regulating the external juridical relations. Hence I am not obliged to let alone what another person declares to be externally his, unless every other person likewise secures me by a guarantee that he will act in relation to what is mine, upon the same principle. This guarantee of reciprocal and mutual abstention from what belongs to others does not require a special juridical act for its establishment, but is already involved in the conception of an external obligation of right, on account of the universality and consequently the reciprocity of the obligatoriness arising from a universal Rule. Now a single will, in relation to an external and consequently contingent possession, cannot serve as a compulsory law for all, because that would be to do violence to the freedom which is in accordance with universal laws. Therefore it is only a will that binds every one, and as such a common, collective, and authoritative will, that can furnish a guarantee of security to all. But the state of men under a universal, external, and public legislation, conjoined with authority and power, is called the civil state. There can therefore be an external mine and thine only in the civil state of society.

Consequence.- It follows, as a corollary, that, if it is juridically possible to have an external object as one's own, the individual subject of possession must be allowed to compel or constrain every person with whom a dispute as to the mine or thine of such a possession may arise, to enter along with himself into the relations of a civil constitution.

9. There May, However, Be an External Mine and Thine Found as a Fact in the State of Nature, but it is only Provisory.

Natural right in the state of a civil constitution means the forms of right which may be deduced from principles a priori as the conditions of such a constitution. It is therefore not to be infringed by the statutory laws of such a constitution; and accordingly the juridical principle remains in force, that, "Whoever proceeds upon a maxim by which it becomes impossible for me to have an object of the exercise of my will as mine, does me a lesion or injury." For a civil constitution is only the juridical condition under which every one has what is his own merely secured to him, as distinguished from its being specially assigned and determined to him. All guarantee, therefore, assumes that everyone to whom a thing is secured is already in possession of it as his own. Hence, prior to the civil constitution- or apart from it- an external mine and thine must be assumed as possible, and along with it a right to compel everyone with whom we could come into any kind of intercourse to enter with us into a constitution in which what is mine or thine can be secured. There may thus be a possession in expectation or in preparation for such a state of security, as can only be established on the law of the common will; and as it is therefore in accordance with the possibility of such a state, it constitutes a provisory or temporary juridical possession; whereas that possession which is found in reality in the civil state of society will be a peremptory or guaranteed possession. Prior to entering into this state, for which he is naturally prepared, the individual rightfully resists those who will not adapt themselves to it, and who would disturb him in his provisory possession; because, if the will of all except himself were imposing upon him an obligation to withdraw from a certain possession, it would still be only a one-sided or unilateral will, and consequently it would have just as little legal title- which can be properly based only on the universalized will- to contest a claim of right as he would have to assert it. Yet be has the advantage on his side, of being in accord with the conditions requisite to the introduction and institution of a civil form of society. In a word, the mode in which anything external may be held as one's own in the state of nature, is just physical possession with a presumption of right thus far in its favour, that by union of the wills of all in a public legislation it will be made juridical; and in this expectation it holds comparatively, as a kind of potential juridical possession.

This prerogative of right, as arising from the fact of empirical possession, is in accordance with the formula: "It is well for those who are in possession" (Beati possidentes). It does not consist in the fact that, because the possessor has the presumption of being a rightful man, it is unnecessary for him to bring forward proof that he possesses a certain thing rightfully, for this position applies only to a case of disputed right. But it is because it accords with the postulate of the practical reason, that everyone is invested with the faculty of having as his own any external object upon which he has exerted his will; and, consequently, all actual possession is a state whose rightfulness is established upon that postulate by an anterior act of will. And such an act, if there be no prior possession of the same object by another opposed to it, does, therefore, provisionally justify and entitle me, according to the law of external freedom, to restrain anyone who refuses to enter with me into a state of public legal freedom from all pretension to the use of such an object. For such a procedure is requisite, in conformity with the postulate of reason, in order to subject to my proper use a thing which would otherwise be practically annihilated, as regards all proper use of it.

FIRST PART. PRIVATE RIGHT.
The System of those Laws Which Require No External Promulgation.
CHAPTER II. The Mode of Acquiring Anything External.
10. The General Principle of External Acquisition.

I acquire a thing when I act (efficio) so that it becomes mine. An external thing is originally mine when it is mine even without the intervention of a juridical act. An acquisition is original and primary when it is not derived from what another had already made his own.

There is nothing external that is as such originally mine; but anything external may be originally acquired when it is an object that no other person has yet made his. A state in which the mine and thine are in common cannot be conceived as having been at any time original. Such a state of things would have to be acquired by an external juridical act, although there may be an original and common possession of an external object. Even if we think hypothetically of a state in which the mine and thine would be originally in common as a communio mei et tui originaria, it would still have to be distinguished from a primeval communion (communio primaeva) with things in common, sometimes supposed to be founded in the first period of the relations of right among men, and which could not be regarded as based upon principles like the former, but only upon history. Even under that condition the historic communio, as a supposed primeval community, would always have to be viewed as acquired and derivative (communio derivativa).

The principle of external acquisition, then, may be expressed thus: "Whatever I bring under my power according to the law of external freedom, of which as an object of my free activity of will I have the capability of making use according to the postulate of the practical reason, and which I will to become mine in conformity with the idea of a possible united common will, is mine."

The practical elements (momenta attendenda) constitutive of the process of original acquisition are:

1. Prehension or seizure of an object which belongs to no one; for, if it belonged already to some one, the act would conflict with the freedom of others, that is, according to universal laws. This is the taking possession of an object of my free activity of will in space and time; the possession, therefore, into which I thus put myself is sensible or physical possession (possessio phenomenon);

2. Declaration of the possession of this object by formal designation and the act of my freewill in interdicting every other person from using it as his;

3. Appropriation, as the act, in idea, of an externally legislative common will, by which all and each are obliged to respect and act in conformity with my act of will.

The validity of the last element in the process of acquisition, as that on which the conclusion that "the external object is mine" rests, is what makes the possession valid as a purely rational and juridical possession (possessio noumenon). It is founded upon the fact that, as all these acts are juridical, they consequently proceed from the practical reason, and therefore, in the question as to what is right, abstraction may be made of the empirical conditions involved, and the conclusion, "the external object is mine," thus becomes a correct inference from the external fact of sensible possession to the internal right of rational possession.

The original primary acquisition of an external object of the action of the will, is called occupancy. It can only take place in reference to substances or corporeal things. Now when this occupation of an external object does take place, the act presupposes, as a condition of such empirical possession, its priority in time before the act of any other who may also be willing to enter upon occupation of it. Hence the legal maxim: "qui prior tempore, potior jure." Such occupation as original or primary is, further, the effect only of a single or unilateral will; for were a bilateral or twofold will requisite for it, it would be derived from a contract of two or more persons with each other, and consequently it would be based upon what another or others had already made their own. It is not easy to see how such an act of free-will as this would be could really form a foundation for every one having his own. However, the first acquisition of a thing is on that account not quite exactly the same as the original acquisition of it. For the acquisition of a public juridical state by union of the wills of all in a universal legislation would be such an original acquisition, seeing that no other of the kind could precede it, and yet it would be derived from the particular wills of all the individuals, and consequently become all-sided or omnilateral; for a properly primary acquisition can only proceed from an individual or unilateral or unilateral will.

DIVISION OF THE SUBJECT OF THE ACQUISITION OF THE EXTERNAL MINE AND THINE.

I. In respect of the matter of object of acquisition, I acquire either a corporeal thing (substance), or the performance of something by another (causality), or this other as a person in respect of his state, so far as I have a right to dispose of the same (in a relation of reciprocity with him).

II. In respect of the form or mode of acquisition, it is either a real right (jus reale), or a personal right (jus personale), or a real-personal right (jus realiter personale), to the possession although not to the use, of another person as if he were a thing.

III. In respect of the ground of right or the title (titulus) of acquisition- which, properly, is not a particular member of the division of rights, but rather a constituent element of the mode of exercising them- anything external is acquired by a certain free exercise of will that is either unilateral, as the act of a single will (facto), or bilateral, as the act of two wills (pacto), or omnilateral, as the act of all the wills of a community together (lege).

SECTION I. Principles of Real Right.

11. What is a Real Right?

The usual definition of real right, or "right in a thing" (jus reale, jus in re), is that "it is a right as against every possessor of it." This is a correct nominal definition. But what is it that entitles me to claim an external object from any one who may appear as its possessor, and to compel him, per vindicationem, to put me again, in place of himself, into possession of it? Is this external juridical relation of my will a kind of immediate relation to an external thing? If so, whoever might think of his right as referring not immediately to persons but to things would have to represent it, although only in an obscure way, somewhat thus. A right on one side has always a duty corresponding to it on the other, so that an external thing, although away from the hands of its first possessor, continues to be still connected with him by a continuing obligation; and thus it refuses to fall under the claim of any other possessor, because it is already bound to another. In this way my right, viewed as a kind of good genius accompanying a thing and preserving it from all external attack, would refer an alien possessor always to me! It is, however, absurd to think of an obligation of persons towards things, and conversely; although it may be allowed in any particular case to represent the juridical relation by a sensible image of this kind, and to express it in this way.

The real definition would run thus: "Right in a thing is a right to the private use of a thing, of which I am in possession- original or derivative- in common with all others." For this is the one condition under which it is alone possible that I can exclude every others possessor from the private use of the thing (jus contra quemlibet hujus rei possessorem). For, except by presupposing such a common collective possession, it cannot be conceived how, when I am not in actual possession of a thing, I could be injured or wronged by others who are in possession of it and use it. By an individual act of my own will I cannot oblige any other person to abstain from the use of a thing in respect of which he would otherwise be under no obligation; and, accordingly, such an obligation can only arise from the collective will of all united in a relation of common possession. Otherwise, I would have to think of a right in a thing, as if the thing has an obligation towards me, and as if the right as against every possessor of it had to be derived from this obligation in the thing, which is an absurd way of representing the subject.

Further, by the term real right (jus reale) is meant not only the right in a thing (jus in re), but also the constitutive principle of all the laws which relate to the real mine and thine. It is, however, evident that a man entirely alone upon the earth could properly neither have nor acquire any external thing as his own; because, between him as a person and all external things as material objects, there could be no relations of obligation. There is therefore, literally, no direct right in a thing, but only that right is to be properly called "real" which belongs to any one as constituted against a person, who is in common possession of things with all others in the civil state of society.

12. The First Acquisition of a Thing can only
be that of the Soil.

By the soil is understood all habitable Land. In relation to everything that is moveable upon it, it is to be regarded as a substance, and the mode of the existence of the moveables is viewed as an inherence in it. And just as, in the theoretical acceptance, accidents cannot exist apart from their substances, so, in the practical relation, moveables upon the soil cannot be regarded as belonging to any one unless he is supposed to have been previously in juridical possession of the soil, so that it is thus considered to be his.

For, let it be supposed that the soil belongs to no one. Then I would be entitled to remove every moveable thing found upon it from its place, even to total loss of it, in order to occupy that place, without infringing thereby on the freedom of any other; there being, by the hypothesis, no possessor of it at all. But everything that can be destroyed, such as a tree, a house, and such like- as regards its matter at least- is moveable; and if we call a thing which cannot be moved without destruction of its form an immoveable, the mine and thine in it is not understood as applying to its substance, but to that which is adherent to it and which does not essentially constitute the thing itself.

13. Every Part of the Soil may be Originally Acquired; and

the Principle of the Possibility of such Acquisition
is the Original Community of the Soil Generally.

The first clause of this proposition is founded upon the postulate of the practical reason (SS 2); the second is established by the following proof.

All men are originally and before any juridical act of will in rightful possession of the soil; that is, they have a right to be wherever nature or chance has placed them without their will. Possession (possessio), which is to be distinguished from residential settlement (sedes) as a voluntary, acquired, and permanent possession, becomes common possession, on account of the connection with each other of all the places on the surface of the earth as a globe. For, had the surface of the earth been an infinite plain, men could have been so dispersed upon it that they might not have come into any necessary communion with each other, and a state of social community would not have been a necessary consequence of their existence upon the earth. Now that possession proper to all men upon the earth, which is prior to all their particular juridical acts, constitutes an original possession in common (communio possessionis originaria). The conception of such an original, common possession of things is not derived from experience, nor is it dependent on conditions of time, as is the case with the imaginary and indemonstrable fiction of a primaeval community of possession in actual history. Hence it is a practical conception of reason, involving in itself the only principle according to which men may use the place they happen to occupy on the surface of the earth, in accordance with laws of right.

14. The Juridical Act of this Original
Acquisition is Occupancy.

The act of taking possession (apprehensio), being at its beginning the physical appropriation of a corporeal thing in space (possessionis physicae), can accord with the law of the external freedom of all, under no other condition than that of its priority in respect of time. In this relation it must have the characteristic of a first act in the way of taking possession, as a free exercise of will. The activity of will, however, as determining that the thing- in this case a definite separate place on the surface of the earth- shall be mine, being an act of appropriation, cannot be otherwise in the case of original acquisition than individual or unilateral (voluntas unilateralis s. propria). Now, occupancy is the acquisition of an external object by an individual act of will. The original acquisition of such an object as a limited portion of the soil can therefore only be accomplished by an act of occupation.

The possibility of this mode of acquisition cannot be intuitively apprehended by pure reason in any way, nor established by its principles, but is an immediate consequence from the postulate of the practical reason. The will as practical reason, however, cannot justify external acquisition otherwise than only in so far as it is itself included in an absolutely authoritative will, with which it is united by implication; or, in other words, only in so far as it is contained within a union of the wills of all who come into practical relation with each other. For an individual, unilateral will- and the same applies to a dual or other particular will- cannot impose on all an obligation which is contingent in itself. This requires an omnilateral or universal will, which is not contingent, but a priori, and which is therefore necessarily united and legislative. Only in accordance with such a principle can there be agreement of the active free-will of each individual with the freedom of all, and consequently rights in general, or even the possibility of an external mine and thine.

15. It is Only within a Civil Constitution that Anything can be Acquired Peremptorily, whereas in the State of Nature Acquisition can only be Provisory.

A civil constitution is objectively necessary as a duty, although subjectively its reality is contingent. Hence, there is connected with it a real natural law of right, to which all external acquisition is subjected.

The empirical title of acquisition has been shown to be constituted by the taking physical possession (apprehensio physica) as founded upon an original community of right in all to the soil. And because a possession in the phenomenal sphere of sense can only be subordinated to that possession which is in accordance with rational conceptions of right, there must correspond to this physical act of possession a rational mode of taking possession by elimination of all the empirical conditions in space and time. This rational form of possession establishes the proposition that "whatever I bring under my power in accordance with laws of external freedom, and will that it shall be mine, becomes mine."

The rational title of acquisition can therefore only lie originally in the idea of the will of all united implicitly, or necessarily to be united, which is here tacitly assumed as an indispensable condition (conditio sine qua non). For by a single will there cannot be imposed upon others an obligation by which they would not have been otherwise bound. But the fact formed by wills actually and universally united in a legislation constitutes the civil state of society. Hence, it is only in conformity with the idea of a civil state of society, or in reference to it and its realization, that anything external can be acquired. Before such a state is realized, and in anticipation of it, acquisition, which would otherwise be derived, is consequently only provisory. The acquisition which is peremptory finds place only in the civil state.

Nevertheless, such provisory acquisition is real acquisition. For, according to the postulate of the juridically practical reason, the possibility of acquisition in whatever state men may happen to be living beside one another, and therefore in the state of nature as well, is a principle of private right. And in accordance with this principle, every one is justified or entitled to exercise that compulsion by which it alone becomes possible to pass out of the state of nature and to enter into that state of civil society which alone can make all acquisition peremptory.

It is a question as to how far the right of taking possession of the soil extends. The answer is, So far as the capability of having it under one's power extends; that is, just as far as he who wills to appropriate it can defend it, as if the soil were to say: "If you cannot protect me, neither can you command me." In this way the controversy about what constitutes a free or closed sea must be decided. Thus, within the range of a cannon-shot no one has a right to intrude on the coast of a country that already belongs to a certain state, in order to fish or gather amber on the shore, or such like. Further, the question is put, "Is cultivation of the soil, by building, agriculture, drainage, etc., necessary in order to its acquisition?" No. For, as these processes as forms of specification are only accidents, they do not constitute objects of immediate possession and can only belong to the subject in so far as the substance of them has been already recognized as his. When it is a question of the first acquisition of a thing, the cultivation or modification of it by labour forms nothing more than an external sign of the fact that it has been taken into possession, and this can be indicated by many other signs that cost less trouble. Again: "May any one be hindered in the act of taking possession, so that neither one nor other of two competitors shall acquire the right of priority, and the soil in consequence may remain for all time free as belonging to no one?" Not at all. Such a hindrance cannot be allowed to take place, because the second of the two, in order to be enabled to do this, would himself have to be upon some neighbouring soil, where he also, in this manner, could be hindered from being, and such absolute hindering would involve a contradiction. It would, however, be quite consistent with the right of occupation, in the case of a certain intervening piece of the soil, to let it lie unused as a neutral ground for the separation of two neighbouring states; but under such a condition, that ground would actually belong to them both in common, and would not be without an owner (res nullius), just because it would be used by both in order to form a separation between them. Again: "May one have a thing as his, on a soil of which no one has appropriated any part as his own?" Yes. In Mongolia, for example, any one may let lie whatever baggage he has, or bring back the horse that has run away from him into his possession as his own, because the whole soil belongs to the people generally, and the use of it accordingly belongs to every individual. But that any one can have a moveable thing on the soil of another as his own is only possible by contract. Finally, there is the question: "May one of two neighbouring nations or tribes resist another when attempting to impose upon them a certain mode of using a particular soil; as, for instance, a tribe of hunters making such an attempt in relation to a pastoral people, or the latter to agriculturists and such like?" Certainly. For the mode in which such peoples or tribes may settle themselves upon the surface of the earth, provided they keep within their own boundaries, is a matter of mere pleasure and choice on their own part (res merae facultatis).

As a further question, it may be asked whether, when neither nature nor chance, but merely our own will, brings us into the neighbourhood of a people that gives no promise of a prospect of entering into civil union with us, we are to be considered entitled in any case to proceed with force in the intention of founding such a union, and bringing into a juridical state such men as the savage American Indians, the Hottentots, and the New Hollanders; or- and the case is not much better- whether we may establish colonies by deceptive purchase, and so become owners of their soil, and, in general, without regard to their first possession, make use at will of our superiority in relation to them? Further, may it not be held that Nature herself, as abhorring a vacuum, seems to demand such a procedure, and that large regions in other continents, that are now magnificently peopled, would otherwise have remained unpossessed by civilized inhabitants and might have for ever remained thus, so that the end of creation would have so far been frustrated? It is almost unnecessary to answer; for it is easy to see through all this flimsy veil of injustice, which just amounts to the Jesuitism of making a good end justify any means. This mode of acquiring the soil is, therefore, to be repudiated.

The indefiniteness of external acquirable objects in respect of their quantity, as well as their quality, makes the problem of the sole primary external acquisition of them one of the most difficult to solve. There must, however, be some one first acquisition of an external object; for every Acquisition cannot be derivative. Hence, the problem is not to be given up as insoluble or in itself as impossible. If it is solved by reference to the original contract, unless this contract is extended so as to include the whole human race, acquisition under it would still remain but provisional.

16. Exposition of the Conception of a Primary
Acquisition of the Soil.

All men are originally in a common collective possession of the soil of the whole earth (communio fundi originaria), and they have naturally each a will to use it (lex justi). But on account of the opposition of the free will of one to that of the other in the sphere of action, which is inevitable by nature, all use of the soil would be prevented did not every will contain at the same time a law for the regulation of the relation of all wills in action, according to which a particular possession can be determined to every one upon the common soil. This is the juridical law (lex juridica). But the distributive law of the mine and thine, as applicable to each individual on the soil, according to the axiom of external freedom, cannot proceed otherwise than from a primarily united will a priori- which does not presuppose any juridical act as requisite for this union. This Law can only take form in the civil state (lex justitiae distributivae); as it is in this state alone that the united common will determines what is right, what is rightful, and what is the constitution of Right. In reference to this state, however- and prior to its establishment and in view of it- it is provisorily a duty for every one to proceed according to the law of external acquisition; and accordingly it is a juridical procedure on the part of the will to lay every one under obligation to recognise the act of possessing and appropriating, although it be only unilaterally. Hence a provisory acquisition of the soil, with all its juridical consequences, is possible in the state of nature.

Such an acquisition, however, requires and also obtains the favour of a permissive law (lex permissiva), in respect of the determination of the limits of juridically possible possession. For it precedes the juridical state, and as merely introductory to it is not yet peremptory; and this favour does not extend farther than the date of the consent of the other co-operators in the establishment of the civil state. But if they are opposed to entering into the civil state, as long as this opposition lasts it carries all the effect of a guaranteed juridical acquisition with it, because the advance from the state of nature to the civil state is founded upon a duty.

17. Deduction of the Conception of the Original
Primary Acquisition.

We have found the title of acquisition in a universal original community of the soil, under the conditions of an external acquisition in space; and the mode of acquisition is contained in the empirical fact of taking possession (apprehensio), conjoined with the will to have an external object as one's own. It is further necessary to unfold, from the principles of the pure juridically practical reason involved in the conception, the juridical acquisition proper of an object- that is, the external mine and thine that follows from the two previous conditions, as rational possession (possessio noumenon).

The juridical conception of the external mine and thine, so far as it involves the category of substance, cannot by "that which is external to me" mean merely "in a place other than that in which I am"; for it is a rational conception. As under the conceptions of the reason only intellectual conceptions can be embraced, the expression in question can only signify "something that is different and distinct from me" according to the idea of a non-empirical possession through, as it were, a continuous activity in taking possession of an external object; and it involves only the notion of having something in my power, which indicates the connection of an object with myself, as a subjective condition of the possibility of making use of it. This forms a purely intellectual conception of the understanding. Now we can leave out or abstract from the sensible conditions of possession, as relations of a person to objects which have no obligation. This process of elimination just gives the rational relation of a person to persons; and it is such that he can bind them all by an obligation in reference to the use of things through his act of will, so far as it is conformable to the axiom of freedom, the postulate of right, and the universal legislation of the common will, conceived as united a priori. This is therefore the rational intelligible possession of things as by pure right, although they are objects of sense.

It is evident that the first modification, limitation, or transformation generally, of a portion of the soil cannot of itself furnish a title to its acquisition, since possession of an accident does not form a ground for legal possession of the substance. Rather, conversely, the inference as to the mine and thine must be drawn from ownership of the substance according to the rule: Accessarium sequitur suum principale. Hence one who has spent labour on a piece of ground that was not already his own, has lost his effort and work to the former owner. This position is so evident of itself that the old opinion to the opposite effect, that is still spread far and wide, can hardly be ascribed to any other than the prevailing illusion which unconsciously leads to the personification of things; and, then, as if they could be bound under an obligation by the labour bestowed upon them to be at the service of the person who does the labour, to regard them as his by immediate right. Otherwise it is probable that the natural question- already discussed- would not have been passed over with so light a tread, namely: "How is a right in a thing possible?" For, right as against every possible possessor of a thing means only the claim of a particular will to the use of an object so far as it may be included in the all-comprehending universal will, and can be thought as in harmony with its law.

As regards bodies situated upon a piece of ground which is already mine, if they otherwise belong to no other person, they belong to me without my requiring any particular juridical act for the purpose of this acquisition; they are mine not facto, but lege. For they may be regarded as accidents inhering in the substance of the soil, and they are thus mine jure rei meae. To this category also belongs everything which is so connected with anything of mine that it cannot be separated from what is mine without altering it substantially. Examples of this are gilding on an object, mixture of a material belonging to me with other things, alluvial deposit, or even alteration of the adjoining bed of a stream or river in my favour so as to produce an increase of my land, etc. By the same principles, the question must also be decided as to whether the acquirable soil may extend farther than the existing land, so as even to include part of the bed of the sea, with the right to fish on my own shores, to gather amber and such like. So far as I have the mechanical capability from my own site, as the place I occupy, to secure my soil from the attack of others- and, therefore, as far as cannon can carry from the shore- all is included in my possession, and the sea is thus far closed (mare clausum). But as there is no site for occupation upon the wide sea itself, possible possession cannot be extended so far, and the open sea is free (mare liberum). But in the case of men, or things that belong to them, becoming stranded on the shore, since the fact is not voluntary, it cannot be regarded by the owner of the shore as giving him a right of acquisition. For shipwreck is not an act of will, nor is its result a lesion to him; and things which may have come thus upon his soil, as still belonging to some one, are not to be treated as being without an owner or res nullius. On the other hand, a river, so far as possession of the bank reaches, may be originally acquired, like any other piece of ground, under the above restrictions, by one who is in possession of both its banks.

PROPERTY.

An external object, which in respect of its substance can be claimed by some one as his own, is called the property (dominium) of that person to whom all the rights in it as a thing belong- like the accidents inhering in a substance- and which, therefore, he as the proprietor (dominus) can dispose of at will (jus disponendi de re sua). But from this it follows at once that such an object can only be a corporeal thing towards which there is no direct personal obligation. Hence a man may be his own master (sui juris) but not the proprietor of himself (sui dominus), so as to be able to dispose of himself at will, to say nothing of the possibility of such a relation to other men; because he is responsible to humanity in his own person. This point, however, as belonging to the right of humanity as such, rather than to that of individual men, would not be discussed at its proper place here, but is only mentioned incidentally for the better elucidation of what has just been said. It may be further observed that there may be two full proprietors of one and the same thing, without there being a mine and thine in common, but only in so far as they are common possessors of what belongs only to one of them as his own. In such a case the whole possession, without the use of the thing, belongs to one only of the co-proprietors (condomini); while to the others belongs all the use of the thing along with its possession. The former as the direct proprietor (dominus directus), therefore, restricts the latter as the proprietor in use (dominus utilis) to the condition of a certain continuous performance, with reference to the thing itself, without limiting him in the use of it.

SECTION II. Principles of Personal Right.

18. Nature and Acquisition of Personal Right.

The possession of the active free-will of another person, as the power to determine it by my will to a certain action, according to laws of freedom, is a form of right relating to the external mine and thine, as affected by the causality of another. It is possible to have several such rights in reference to the same person or to different persons. The principle of the system of laws, according to which I can be in such possession, is that of personal right, and there is only one such principle.

The acquisition of a personal right can never be primary or arbitrary; for such a mode of acquiring it would not be in accordance with the principle of the harmony of the freedom of my will with the freedom of every other, and it would therefore be wrong. Nor can such a right be acquired by means of any unjust act of another (facto injusti alterius), as being itself contrary to right; for if such a wrong as it implies were perpetrated on me, and I could demand satisfaction from the other, in accordance with right, yet in such a case I would only be entitled to maintain undiminished what was mine, and not to acquire anything more than what I formerly had.

Acquisition by means of the action of another, to which I determine his will according to laws of right, is therefore always derived from what that other has as his own. This derivation, as a juridical act, cannot be effected by a mere negative relinquishment or renunciation of what is his (per derelictionem aut renunciationem); because such a negative act would only amount to a cessation of his right, and not to the acquirement of a right on the part of another. It is therefore only by positive transference (translatio), or conveyance, that a personal right can be acquired; and this is only possible by means of a common will, through which objects come into the power of one or other, so that as one renounces a particular thing which he holds under the common right, the same object when accepted by another, in consequence of a positive act of will, becomes his. Such transference of the property of one to another is termed its alienation. The act of the united wills of two persons, by which what belonged to one passes to the other, constitutes contract.

19. Acquisition by Contract.

In every contract there are four juridical acts of will involved; two of them being preparatory acts, and two of them constitutive acts. The two preparatory acts, as forms of treating in the transaction, are offer (oblatio) and approval (approbatio); the two constitutive acts, as the forms of concluding the transaction, are promise (promissum) and acceptance (acceptatio). For an offer cannot constitute a promise before it can be judged that the thing offered (oblatum) is something that is agreeable to the party to whom it is offered, and this much is shown by the first two declarations; but by them alone there is nothing as yet acquired.

Further, it is neither by the particular will of the promiser nor that of the acceptor that the property of the former passes over to the latter. This is effected only by the combined or united wills of both, and consequently so far only as the will of both is declared at the same time or simultaneously. Now, such simultaneousness is impossible by empirical acts of declaration, which can only follow each other in time and are never actually simultaneous. For if I have promised, and another person is now merely willing to accept, during the interval before actual acceptance, however short it may be, I may retract my offer, because I am thus far still free; and, on the other side, the acceptor, for the same reason, may likewise hold himself not to be bound, up till the moment of acceptance, by his counter-declaration following upon the promise. The external formalities or solemnities (solemnia) on the conclusion of a contract- such as shaking hands or breaking a straw (stipula) laid hold of by two persons- and all the various modes of confirming the declarations on either side, prove in fact the embarrassment of the contracting parties as to how and in what way they may represent declarations, which are always successive, as existing simultaneously at the same moment; and these forms fail to do this. They are, by their very nature, acts necessarily following each other in time, so that when the one act is, the other either is not yet or is no longer.

It is only the philosophical transcendental deduction of the conception of acquisition by contract that can remove all these difficulties. In a juridical external relation, my taking possession of the free-will of another, as the cause that determined it to a certain act, is conceived at first empirically by means of the declaration and counter-declaration of the free-will of each of us in time, as the sensible conditions of taking possession; and the two juridical acts must necessarily be regarded as following one another in time. But because this relation, viewed as juridical, is purely rational in itself, the will as a law-giving faculty of reason represents this possession as intelligible or rational (possessio noumenon), in accordance with conceptions of freedom and under abstraction of those empirical conditions. And now, the two acts of promise and acceptance are not regarded as following one another in time, but, in the manner of a pactum re initum, as proceeding from a common will, which is expressed by the term "at the same time," or "simultaneous," and the object promised (promissum) is represented, under elimination of empirical conditions, as acquired according to the law of the pure practical reason.

That this is the true and only possible deduction of the idea of acquisition by contract is sufficiently attested by the laborious yet always futile striving of writers on jurisprudence such as Moses Mendelssohn in his Jerusalem- to adduce a proof of its rational possibility. The question is put thus: "Why ought I to keep my Promise?" For it is assumed as understood by all that I ought to do so. It is, however, absolutely impossible to give any further proof of the categorical imperative implied; just as it is impossible for the geometrician to prove by rational syllogisms that in order to construct a triangle I must take three lines- so far an analytical proposition- of which three lines any two together must be greater than the third- a synthetical proposition, and like the former a priori. It is a postulate of the pure reason that we ought to abstract from all the sensible conditions of space and time in reference to the conception of right; and the theory of the possibility of such abstraction from these conditions, without taking away the reality of the possession, just constitutes the transcendental deduction of the conception of acquisition by contract. It is quite akin to what was presented under the last title, as the theory of acquisition by occupation of the external object.

20. What is Acquired by Contract.

But what is that, designated as external, which I acquire by contract? As it is only the causality of the active will of another, in respect of the performance of something promised to me, I do not immediately acquire thereby an external thing, but an act of the will in question, whereby a thing is brought under my power so that I make it mine. By the contract, therefore, I acquire the promise of another, as distinguished from the thing promised; and yet something is thereby added to my having and possession. I have become the richer in possession (locupletior) by the acquisition of an active obligation that I can bring to bear upon the freedom and capability of another. This my right, however, is only a personal right, valid only to the effect of acting upon a particular physical person and specially upon the causality of his will, so that he shall perform something for me. It is not a real right upon that moral person, which is identified with the idea of the united will of all viewed a priori, and through which alone I can acquire a right valid against every possessor of the thing. For, it is in this that all right in a thing consists.

The transfer or transmission of what is mine to another by contract, takes place according to the law of continuity (lex continui). Possession of the object is not interrupted for a moment during this act; for, otherwise, I would acquire an object in this state as a thing that had no possessor, and it would thus be acquired originally, which is contrary to the idea of a contract. This continuity, however, implies that it is not the particular will of either the promiser or the acceptor, but their united will in common, that transfers what is mine to another. And hence it is not accomplished in such a manner that the promiser first relinquishes (derelinquit) his possession for the benefit of another, or renounces his right (renunciat), and thereupon the other at the same time enters upon it; or conversely. The transfer (translatio) is therefore an act in which the object belongs for a moment at the same time to both, just as in the parabolic path of a projectile the object on reaching its highest point may be regarded for a moment as at the same time both rising and falling, and as thus passing in fact from the ascending to the falling motion.

21. Acceptance and Delivery.

A thing is not acquired in a case of contract by the acceptance (acceptatio) of the promise, but only by the delivery (traditio) of the object promised. For all promise is relative to performance; and if what was promised is a thing, the performance cannot be executed otherwise than by an act whereby the acceptor is put by the promiser into possession of the thing; and this is delivery. Before the delivery and the reception of the thing, the performance of the act required has not yet taken place; the thing has not yet passed from the one person to the other and, consequently, has not been acquired by that other. Hence the right arising from a contract is only a personal right; and it only becomes a real right by delivery.

A contract upon which delivery immediately follows (pactum re initum) excludes any interval of time between its conclusion and its execution; and as such it requires no further particular act in the future by which one person may transfer to another what is his. But if there is a time- definite or indefinite- agreed upon between them for the delivery, the question then arises whether the thing has already before that time become the acceptor's by the contract, so that his right is a right in the thing; or whether a further special contract regarding the delivery alone must be entered upon, so that the right that is acquired by mere acceptance is only a personal right, and thus it does not become a right in the thing until delivery? That the relation must be determined according to the latter alternative will be clear from what follows.

Suppose I conclude a contract about a thing that I wish to acquire- such as a horse- and that I take it immediately into my stable, or otherwise into my possession; then it is mine (vi pacti re initi), and my right is a right in the thing. But if I leave it in the hands of the seller without arranging with him specially in whose physical possession or holding (detentio) this thing shall be before my taking possession of it (apprehensio), and consequently, before the actual change of possession, the horse is not yet mine; and the right which I acquire is only a right against a particular person- namely, the seller of the horse- to be put into possession of the object (poscendi traditionem) as the subjective condition of any use of it at my will. My right is thus only a personal right to demand from the seller the performance of his promise (praestatio) to put me into possession of the thing. Now, if the contract does not contain the condition of delivery at the same time- as a pactum re initum- and consequently an interval of time intervenes between the conclusion of the contract and the taking possession of the object of acquisition, I cannot obtain possession of it during this interval otherwise than by exercising the particular juridical activity called a possessory act (actum possessorium), which constitutes a special contract. This act consists in my saying, "I will send to fetch the horse," to which the seller has to agree. For it is not self-evident or universally reasonable that any one will take a thing destined for the use of another into his charge at his own risk. On the contrary, a special contract is necessary for this arrangement, according to which the alienator of a thing continues to be its owner during a certain definite time, and must bear the risk of whatever may happen to it; while the acquirer can only be regarded by the seller as the owner when he has delayed to enter into possession beyond the date at which he agreed to take delivery. Prior to the possessory act, therefore, all that is acquired by the contract is only a personal right; and the acceptor can acquire an external thing only by delivery.

SECTION III. Principles of Personal Right that is Real in Kind. (Jus Realiter Personale).

22. Nature of Personal Right of a Real Kind.

Personal right of a real kind is the right to the possession of an external object as a thing, and to the use of it as a person. The mine and thine embraced under this right relate specially to the family and household; and the relations involved are those of free beings in reciprocal real interaction with each other. Through their relations and influence as persons upon one another, in accordance with the principle of external freedom as the cause of it, they form a society composed as a whole of members standing in community with each other as persons; and this constitutes the household. The mode in which this social status is acquired by individuals, and the functions which prevail within it, proceed neither by arbitrary individual action (facto), nor by mere contract (pacto), but by law (lege). And this law as being not only a right, but also as constituting possession in reference to a person, is a right rising above all mere real and personal right. It must, in fact, form the right of humanity in our own person; and, as such, it has as its consequence a natural permissive law, by the favour of which such acquisition becomes possible to us.

23. What is acquired in the household.

The acquisition that is founded upon this law is, as regards its objects, threefold. The man acquires a wife; the husband and wife acquire children, constituting a family; and the family acquire domestics. All these objects, while acquirable, are inalienable; and the right of possession in these objects is the most strictly personal of all rights.

The Rights of the Family as a Domestic Society

Title I. Conjugal Right. (Husband and Wife)

24. The Natural Basis of Marriage.

The domestic relations are founded on marriage, and marriage is founded upon the natural reciprocity or intercommunity (commercium) of the sexes.* This natural union of the sexes proceeds according to the mere animal nature (vaga libido, venus vulgivaga, fornicatio), or according to the law. The latter is marriage (matrimonium), which is the union of two persons of different sex for life-long reciprocal possession of their sexual faculties. The end of producing and educating children may be regarded as always the end of nature in implanting mutual desire and inclination in the sexes; but it is not necessary for the rightfulness of marriage that those who marry should set this before themselves as the end of their union, otherwise the marriage would be dissolved of itself when the production of children ceased.

*Commercium sexuale est usus membrorum et facultatum sexualium alterius. This "usus" is either natural, by which human beings may reproduce their own kind, or unnatural, which, again, refers either to a person of the same sex or to an animal of another species than man. These transgressions of all law, as crimina carnis contra naturam, are even "not to be named"; and, as wrongs against all humanity in the person, they cannot be saved, by any limitation or exception whatever, from entire reprobation.

And even assuming that enjoyment in the reciprocal use of the sexual endowments is an end of marriage, yet the contract of marriage is not on that account a matter of arbitrary will, but is a contract necessary in its nature by the law of humanity. In other words, if a man and a woman have the will to enter on reciprocal enjoyment in accordance with their sexual nature, they must necessarily marry each other; and this necessity is in accordance with the juridical laws of pure reason.

25. The Rational Right of Marriage.

For, this natural commercium- as a usus membrorum sexualium alterius- is an enjoyment for which the one person is given up to the other. In this relation the human individual makes himself a res, which is contrary to the right of humanity in his own person. This, however, is only possible under the one condition, that as the one person is acquired by the other as a res, that same person also equally acquires the other reciprocally, and thus regains and reestablishes the rational personality. The acquisition of a part of the human organism being, on account of its unity, at the same time the acquisition of the whole person, it follows that the surrender and acceptation of, or by, one sex in relation to the other, is not only permissible under the condition of marriage, but is further only really possible under that condition. But the personal right thus acquired is, at the same time, real in kind; and this characteristic of it is established by the fact that if one of the married persons run away or enter into the possession of another, the other is entitled, at any time, and incontestably, to bring such a one back to the former relation, as if that person were a thing.

26. Monogamy and Equality in Marriage.

For the same reasons, the relation of the married persons to each other is a relation of equality as regards the mutual possession of their persons, as well as of their goods. Consequently marriage is only truly realized in monogamy; for in the relation of polygamy the person who is given away on the one side, gains only a part of the one to whom that person is given up, and therefore becomes a mere res. But in respect of their goods, they have severally the right to renounce the use of any part of them, although only by a special contract.

From the principle thus stated, it also follows that concubinage is as little capable of being brought under a contract of right as the hiring of a person on any one occasion, in the way of a pactum fornicationis. For, as regards such a contract as this latter relation would imply, it must be admitted by all that any one who might enter into it could not be legally held to the fulfillment of their promise if they wished to resile from it. And as regards the former, a contract of concubinage would also fall as a pactum turpe; because as a contract of the hire (locatio, conductio), of a part for the use of another, on account of the inseparable unity of the members of a person, any one entering into such a contract would be actually surrendering as a res to the arbitrary will of another. Hence any party may annul a contract like this if entered into with any other, at any time and at pleasure; and that other would have no ground, in the circumstances, to complain of a lesion of his right. The same holds likewise of a morganatic or "left-hand" marriage, contracted in order to turn the inequality in the social status of the two parties to advantage in the way of establishing the social supremacy of the one over the other; for, in fact, such a relation is not really different from concubinage, according to the principles of natural right, and therefore does not constitute a real marriage. Hence the question may be raised as to whether it is not contrary to the equality of married persons when the law says in any way of the husband in relation to the wife, "he shall be thy master," so that he is represented as the one who commands, and she is the one who obeys. This, however, cannot be regarded as contrary to the natural equality of a human pair, if such legal supremacy is based only upon the natural superiority of the faculties of the husband compared with the wife, in the effectuation of the common interest of the household, and if the right to command is based merely upon this fact. For this right may thus be deduced from the very duty of unity and equality in relation to the end involved.

27. Fulfillment of the Contract of Marriage.

The contract of marriage is completed only by conjugal cohabitation. A contract of two persons of different sex, with the secret understanding either to abstain from conjugal cohabitation or with the consciousness on either side of incapacity for it, is a simulated contract; it does not constitute a marriage, and it may be dissolved by either of the parties at will. But if the incapacity only arises after marriage, the right of the contract is not annulled or diminished by a contingency that cannot be legally blamed.

The acquisition of a spouse, either as a husband or as a wife, is therefore not constituted facto- that is, by cohabitation- without a preceding contract; nor even pacto- by a mere contract of marriage, without subsequent cohabitation; but only lege, that is, as a juridical consequence of the obligation that is formed by two persons entering into a sexual union solely on the basis of a reciprocal possession of each other, which possession at the same time is only effected in reality by the reciprocal usus facultatum sexualium alterius.

Title II. Parental Right. (Parent and Child).

28. The Relation of Parent and Child.

From the duty of man towards himself- that is, towards the humanity in his own person there thus arises a personal right on the part of the members of the opposite sexes, as persons, to acquire one another really and reciprocally by marriage. In like manner, from the fact of procreation in the union thus constituted, there follows the duty of preserving and rearing children as the products of this union. Accordingly, children, as persons, have, at the same time, an original congenital right- distinguished from mere hereditary right- to be reared by the care of their parents till they are capable of maintaining themselves; and this provision becomes immediately theirs by law, without any particular juridical act being required to determine it.

For what is thus produced is a person, and it is impossible to think of a being endowed with personal freedom as produced merely by a physical process. And hence, in the practical relation, it is quite a correct and even a necessary idea to regard the act of generation as a process by which a person is brought without his consent into the world and placed in it by the responsible free will of others. This act, therefore, attaches an obligation to the parents to make their children- as far as their power goes- contented with the condition thus acquired. Hence parents cannot regard their child as, in a manner, a thing of their own making; for a being endowed with freedom cannot be so regarded. Nor, consequently, have they a right to destroy it as if it were their own property, or even to leave it to chance; because they have brought a being into the world who becomes in fact a citizen of the world, and they have placed that being in a state which they cannot be left to treat with indifference, even according to the natural conceptions of right.

We cannot even conceive how it is possible that God can create free beings; for it appears as if all their future actions, being predetermined by that first act, would be contained in the chain of natural necessity, and that, therefore, they could not be free. But as men we are free in fact, as is proved by the categorical imperative in the moral and practical relation as an authoritative decision of reason; yet reason cannot make the possibility of such a relation of cause to effect conceivable from the theoretical point of view, because they are both suprasensible. All that can be demanded of reason under these conditions would merely be to prove that there is no contradiction involved in the conception of a creation of free beings; and this may be done by showing that contradiction only arises when, along with the category of causality, the condition of time is transferred to the relation of suprasensible things. This condition, as implying that the cause of an effect must precede the effect as its reason, is inevitable in thinking the relation of objects of sense to one another; and if this conception of causality were to have objective reality given to it in the theoretical bearing, it would also have to be referred to the suprasensible sphere. But the contradiction vanishes when the pure category, apart from any sensible conditions, is applied from the moral and practical point of view, and consequently as in a non-sensible relation to the conception of creation.

The philosophical jurist will not regard this investigation, when thus carried back even to the ultimate principles of the transcendental philosophy, as an unnecessary subtlety in a metaphysic of morals, or as losing itself in aimless obscurity, when he takes into consideration the difficulty of doing justice in this inquiry to the ultimate relations of the principles of right.

29. The Rights of the Parent.

From the duty thus indicated, there further necessarily arises the right of the parents to the management and training of the child, so long as it is itself incapable of making proper use of its body as an organism, and of its mind as an understanding. This involves its nourishment and the care of its education. This includes, in general, the function of forming and developing it practically, that it may be able in the future to maintain and advance itself, and also its moral culture and development, the guilt of neglecting it falling upon the parents. All this training is to be continued till the child reaches the period of emancipation (emancipatio), as the age of practicable self-support. The parents then virtually renounce the parental right to command, as well as all claim to repayment for their previous care and trouble; for which care and trouble, after the process of education is complete, they can only appeal to the children, by way of any claim, on the ground of the obligation of gratitude as a duty of virtue.

From the fact of personality in the children, it further follows that they can never be regarded as the property of the parents, but only as belonging to them by way of being in their possession, like other things that are held apart from the possession of all others and that can be brought back even against the will of the subjects. Hence the right of the parents is not a purely real right, and it is not alienable (jus personalissimum). But neither is it a merely personal right; it is a personal right of a real kind, that is, a personal right that is constituted and exercised after the manner of a real right.

It is therefore evident that the title of a personal right of a real kind must necessarily be added, in the science of right, to the titles of real right and personal right, the division of rights into these two being not complete. For, if the right of the parents to the children were treated as if it were merely a real right to a part of what belongs to their house, they could not found only upon the duty of the children to return to them in claiming them when they run away, but they would be then entitled to seize them and impound them like things or runaway cattle.

Title III. Household Right. (Master and Servant)

30. Relation and Right of the Master of a Household.

The children of the house, who, along with the parents, constitute a family, attain majority, and become masters of themselves (majorennes, sui juris), even without a contract of release from their previous state of dependence, by their actually attaining to the capability of self-maintenance. This attainment arises, on the one hand, as a state of natural majority, with the advance of years in the general course of nature; and, on the other hand, it takes form, as a state in accordance with their own natural condition. They thus acquire the right of being their own masters, without the interposition of any special juridical act, and therefore merely by law (lege); and they owe their parents nothing by way of legal debt for their education, just as the parents, on their side, are now released from their obligations to the children in the same way. Parents and children thus gain or regain their natural freedom; and the domestic society, which was necessary according to the law of right, is thus naturally dissolved.

Both parties, however, may resolve to continue the household, but under another mode of obligation. It may assume the form of a relation between the head of the house, as its master, and the other members as domestic servants, male or female; and the connection between them in this new regulated domestic economy (societas herilis) may be determined by contract. The master of the house, actually or virtually, enters into contract with the children, now become major and masters of themselves; or, if there be no children in the family, with other free persons constituting the membership of the household; and thus there is established domestic relationship not founded on social equality, but such that one commands as master, and another obeys as servant (imperantis et subjecti domestici).

The domestics or servants may then be regarded by the master of the household as thus far his. As regards the form or mode of his possession of them, they belong to him as if by a real right; for if any of them run away, he is entitled to bring them again under his power by a unilateral act of his will. But as regards the matter of his right, or the use he is entitled to make of such persons as his domestics, he is not entitled to conduct himself towards them as if he was their proprietor or owner (dominus servi); because they are only subjected to his power by contract, and by a contract under certain definite restrictions. For a contract by which the one party renounced his whole freedom for the advantage of the other, ceasing thereby to be a person and consequently having no duty even to observe a contract, is self contradictory, and is therefore of itself null and void. The question as to the right of property in relation to one who has lost his legal personality by a crime does not concern us here.

This contract, then, of the master of a household with his domestics, cannot be of such a nature that the use of them could ever rightly become an abuse of them; and the judgement as to what constitutes use or abuse in such circumstances the is not left merely to the master, but is also competent to the servants, who ought never to be held in bondage or bodily servitude as slaves or serfs. Such a contract cannot, therefore, be concluded for life, but in all cases only for a definite period, within which one party may intimate to the other a termination of their connection. Children, however, including even the children of one who has become enslaved owing to a crime, are always free. For every man is born free, because he has at birth as yet broken no law; and even the cost of his education till his maturity cannot be reckoned as a debt which he is bound to pay. Even a slave, if it were in his power, would be bound to educate his children without being entitled to count and reckon with them for the cost; and in view of his own incapacity for discharging this function, the possessor of a slave, therefore, enters upon the obligation which he has rendered the slave himself unable to fulfil.

Here, again, as under the first two titles, it is clear that there is a personal right of a real kind, in the relation of the master of a house to his domestics. For he can legally demand them as belonging to what is externally his, from any other possessor of them; and he is entitled to fetch them back to his house, even before the reasons that may have led them to run away, and their particular right in the circumstances, have been juridically investigated.

SYSTEMATIC DIVISION OF ALL THE RIGHTS CAPABLE OF BEING ACQUIRED BY CONTRACT.
31. Division of Contracts Juridical Conceptions
of Money and a Book.

It is reasonable to demand that a metaphysical science of right shall completely and definitely determine the members of a logical division of its conceptions a priori, and thus establish them in a genuine system. All empirical division, on the other hand, is merely fragmentary partition, and it leaves us in uncertainty as to whether there may not be more members still required to complete the whole sphere of the divided conception. A division that is made according to a principle a priori may be called, in contrast to all empirical partitions, a dogmatic division.

Every contract, regarded in itself objectively, consists of two juridical acts: the promise and its acceptance. Acquisition by the latter, unless it be a pactum re initum which requires delivery, is not a part, but the juridically necessary consequence of the contract. Considered again subjectively, or as to whether the acquisition, which ought to happen as a necessary consequence according to reason, will also follow, in fact, as a physical consequence, it is evident that I have no security or guarantee that this will happen by the mere acceptance of a promise. There is, therefore, something externally required connected with the mode of the contract, in reference to the certainty of acquisition by it; and this can only be some element completing and determining the means necessary to the attainment of acquisition as realizing the purpose of the contract. And in his connection and behoof, three persons are required to intervene- the promiser, the acceptor, and the cautioner or surety. The importance of the cautioner is evident; but by his intervention and his special contract with the promiser, the acceptor gains nothing in respect of the object but the means of compulsion that enable him to obtain what is his own.

According to these rational principles of logical division, there are properly only three pure and simple modes of contract. There are, however, innumerable mixed and empirical modes, adding statutory and conventional forms to the principles of mine and thine that are in accordance with rational laws. But they lie outside of the circle of the metaphysical science of right, whose rational modes of contract can alone be indicated here.

All contracts are founded upon a purpose of acquisition, and are either:

A. Gratuitous contracts, with unilateral acquisition; or

B. Onerous contracts, with reciprocal acquisition; or

C. Cautionary contracts, with no acquisition, but only guarantee of what has been already acquired. These contracts may be gratuitous on the one side, and yet, at the same time, onerous on the other.

A. The gratuitous contracts (pacta gratuita) are:

1. Depositation (depositum), involving the preservation of some valuable deposited in trust;

2. Commodate (commodatum) a loan of the use of a thing;

3. Donation (donatio), a free gift.

B. The onerous contracts are contracts either of permutation or of hiring.

I. Contracts of permutation or reciprocal exchange (permutatio late sic dicta):

1. Barter, or strictly real exchange (permutatio stricte sic dicta). Goods exchanged for goods.

2. Purchase and sale (emptio venditio). Goods exchanged for money.

3. Loan (mutuum). Loan of a fungible under condition of its being returned in kind: corn for corn, or money for money.

II. Contracts of letting and hiring (locatio conductio):

1. Letting of a thing on hire to another person who is to make use of it (locatio rei). If the thing can only be restored in specie, it may be the subject of an onerous contract combining the consideration of interest with it (pactum usurarium).

2. Letting of work on hire (locatio operae). Consent to the use of my powers by another for a certain price (merces). The worker under this contract is a hired servant (mercenarius).

3. Mandate (mandatum). The contract of mandate is an engagement to perform or execute a certain business in place and in name of another person. If the action is merely done in the place of another, but not, at the same time, in his name, it is performance without commission (gestio negotii); but if it is rightfully performed in name of the other, it constitutes mandate, which as a contract of procuration is an onerous contract (mandatum onerosum).

C. The cautionary contracts (cautiones) are:

1. Pledge (pignus). Caution by a moveable deposited as security.
2. Suretyship (fidejussio). Caution for the fulfillment of the promise of another.
3. Personal security (praestatio obsidis).

Guarantee of personal performance.

This list of all modes in which the property of one person may be transferred or conveyed to another includes conceptions of certain objects or instruments required for such transference (translatio). These appear to be entirely empirical, and it may therefore seem questionable whether they are entitled to a place in a metaphysical science of right. For, in such a science, the divisions must be made according to principles a priori; and hence the matter of the juridical relation, which may be conventional, ought to be left out of account, and only its form should be taken into consideration.

Such conceptions may be illustrated by taking the instance of money, in contradistinction from all other exchangeable things as wares and merchandise; or by the case of a book. And considering these as illustrative examples in this connection, it will be shown that the conception of money as the greatest and most useable of all the means of human intercommunication through things, in the way of purchase and sale in commerce, as well as that of books as the greatest means of carrying on the interchange of thought, resolve themselves into relations that are purely intellectual and rational. And hence it will be made evident that such conceptions do not really detract from the purity of the given scheme of pure rational contracts, by empirical admixture.

Illustration of Relations of Contract by the
Conceptions of Money and a Book

I. What is Money?

Money is a thing which can only be made use of, by being alienated or exchanged. This is a good nominal definition, as given by Achenwall; and it is sufficient to distinguish objects of the will of this kind from all other objects. But it gives us no information regarding the rational possibility of such a thing as money is. Yet we see thus much by the definition: (1) that the alienation in this mode of human intercommunication and exchange is not viewed as a gift, but is intended as a mode of reciprocal acquisition by an onerous contract; and (2) that it is regarded as a mere means of carrying on commerce, universally adopted by the people, but having no value as such of itself, in contrast to other things as mercantile goods or wares which have a particular value in relation to special wants existing among the people. It therefore represents all exchangeable things.

A bushel of corn has the greatest direct value as a means of satisfying human wants. Cattle may be fed by it; and these again are subservient to our nourishment and locomotion, and they even labour in our stead. Thus, by means of corn, men are multiplied and supported, who not only act again in reproducing such natural products, but also by other artificial products they can come to the relief of all our proper wants. Thus are men enabled to build dwellings, to prepare clothing, and to supply all the ingenious comforts and enjoyments which make up the products of industry. On the other hand, the value of money is only indirect. It cannot be itself enjoyed, nor be used directly for enjoyment; it is, however, a means towards this, and of all outward things it is of the highest utility.

We may found a real definition of money provisionally upon these considerations. It may thus be defined as the universal means of carrying on the industry of men in exchanging intercommunications with each other. Hence national wealth, in so far as it can be acquired by means of money, is properly only the sum of the industry or applied labour with which men pay each other, and which is represented by the money in circulation among the people.

The thing which is to be called money must, therefore, have cost as much industry to produce it, or even to put it into the hands of others, as may be equivalent to the industry or labour required for the acquisition of the goods or wares or merchandise, as natural or artificial products, for which it is exchanged. For if it were easier to procure the material which is called money than the goods that are required, there would be more money in the market than goods to be sold; and because the seller would then have to expend more labour upon his goods than the buyer on the equivalent, the money coming in to him more rapidly, the labour applied to the preparation of goods and industry generally, with the industrial productivity which is the source of the public wealth, would at the same time dwindle and be cut down. Hence bank notes and assignations are not to be regarded as money, although they may take its place by way of representing it for a time; because it costs almost no labour to prepare them, and their value is based merely upon the opinion prevailing as to the further continuance of the previous possibility of changing them into ready money. But on its being in any way found out that there is not ready money in sufficient quantity for easy and safe conversion of such notes or assignations, the opinion gives way, and a fall in their value becomes inevitable. Thus the industrial labour of those who work the gold and silver mines in Peru and Mexico- especially on account of the frequent failures in the application of fruitless efforts to discover new veins of these precious metals- is probably even greater than what is expended in the manufacture of goods in Europe. Hence such mining labour, as unrewarded in the circumstances, would be abandoned of itself, and the countries mentioned would in consequence soon sink into poverty, did not the industry of Europe, stimulated in turn by these very metals, proportionally expand at the same time so as constantly to keep up the zeal of the miners in their work by the articles of luxury thereby offered to them. It is thus that the concurrence of industry with industry, and of labour with labour, is always maintained.

But how is it possible that what at the beginning constituted only goods or wares, at length became money? This has happened wherever a sovereign as great and powerful consumer of a particular substance, which he at first used merely for the adornment and decoration of his servants and court, has enforced the tribute of his subjects in this kind of material. Thus it may have been gold, or silver, or copper, or a species of beautiful shells called cowries, or even a sort of mat called makutes, as in Congo; or ingots of iron, as in Senegal; or Negro slaves, as on the Guinea Coast. When the ruler of the country demanded such things as imposts, those whose labour had to be put in motion to procure them were also paid by means of them, according to certain regulations of commerce then established, as in a market or exchange. As it appears to me, it is only thus that a particular species of goods came to be made a legal means of carrying on the industrial labour of the subjects in their commerce with each other, and thereby forming the medium of the national wealth. And thus it practically became money.

The rational conception of money, under which the empirical conception is embraced, is therefore that of a thing which, in the course of the public permutation or exchange of possessions (permutatio publica), determines the price of all the other things that form products or goods- under which term even the sciences are included, in so far as they are not taught gratis to others. The quantity of it among a people constitutes their wealth (opulentia). For price (pretium) is the public judgement about the value of a thing, in relation to the proportionate abundance of what forms the universal representative means in circulation for carrying on the reciprocal interchange of the products of industry or labour.* The precious metals, when they are not merely weighed but also stamped or provided with a sign indicating how much they are worth, form legal money, and are called coin.

*Hence where commerce is extensive neither gold nor copper is specially used as money, but only as constituting wares; because there is too little of the first and too much of the second for them to be easily brought into circulation, so as at once to have the former in such small pieces as are necessary in payment for particular goods and not to have the latter in great quantity in case of the smallest acquisitions. Hence silver- more or less alloyed with copper- is taken as the proper material of money and the measure of the calculation of all prices in the great commercial intercommunications of the world; and the other metals- and still more non-metalic substances- can only take its place in the case of a people of limited commerce.

According to Adam Smith: "Money has become, in all civilized nations, the universal instrument of commerce, by the intervention of which goods of all kinds are bought and sold or exchanged for one another." This definition expands the empirical conception of money to the rational idea of it, by taking regard only to the implied form of the reciprocal performances in the onerous contracts, and thus abstracting from their matter. It is thus conformable to the conception of right in the permutation and exchange of the mine and thine generally (commutatio late sic dicta). The definition, therefore, accords with the representation in the above synopsis of a dogmatic division of contracts a priori, and consequently with the metaphysical principle of right in general.

II. What is a Book?

A book is a writing which contains a discourse addressed by some one to the public, through visible signs of speech. It is a matter of indifference to the present considerations whether it is written by a pen or imprinted by types, and on few or many pages. He who speaks to the public in his own name is the author. He who addresses the writing to the public in the name of the author is the publisher. When a publisher does this with the permission or authority of the author, the act is in accordance with right, and he is the rightful publisher; but if this is done without such permission or authority, the act is contrary to right, and the publisher is a counterfeiter or unlawful publisher. The whole of a set of copies of the original document is called an edition.

The Unauthorized Publishing of Books is Contrary to the
Principles of Right, and is Rightly Prohibited.

A writing is not an immediate direct presentation of a conception, as is the case, for instance, with an engraving that exhibits a portrait, or a bust or cast by a sculptor. It is a discourse addressed in a particular form to the public; and the author may be said to speak publicly by means of his publisher. The publisher, again, speaks by the aid of the printer as his workman (operarius), yet not in his own name, for otherwise he would be the author, but in the name of the author; and he is only entitled to do so in virtue of a mandate given him to that effect by the author. Now the unauthorized printer and publisher speaks by an assumed authority in his publication; in the name indeed of the author, but without a mandate to that effect (gerit se mandatarium absque mandato). Consequently such an unauthorized publication is a wrong committed upon the authorized and only lawful publisher, as it amounts to a pilfering of the profits which the latter was entitled and able to draw from the use of his proper right (furtum usus). Unauthorized printing and publication of books is, therefore, forbidden- as an act of counterfeit and piracy- on the ground of right.

There seems, however, to be an impression that there is a sort of common right to print and publish books; but the slightest reflection must convince any one that this would be a great injustice. The reason of it is found simply in the fact that a book, regarded from one point of view, is an external product of mechanical art (opus mechanicum), that can be imitated by any one who may be in rightful possession of a copy; and it is therefore his by a real right.

But, from another point of view, a book is not merely an external thing, but is a discourse of the publisher to the public, and he is only entitled to do this publicly under the mandate of the author (praestatio operae); and this constitutes a personal right. The error underlying the impression referred to, therefore, arises from an interchange and confusion of these two kinds of right in relation to books.

Confusion of Personal Right and Real Right.

The confusion of personal right with real right may be likewise shown by reference to a difference of view in connection with another contract, falling under the head of contracts of hiring (B II. I), namely, the contract of lease (jus incolatus). The question is raised as to whether a proprietor when he has sold a house or a piece of ground held on lease, before the expiry of the period of lease, was bound to add the condition of the continuance of the lease to the contract of purchase; or whether it should be held that "purchase breaks hire," of course under reservation of a period of warning determined by the nature of the subject in use. In the former view, a house or farm would be regarded as having a burden lying upon it, constituting a real right acquired in it by the lessee; and this might well enough be carried out by a clause merely indorsing or ingrossing the contract of lease in the deed of sale. But as it would no longer then be a simple lease; another contract would properly be required to be conjoined, a matter which few lessors would be disposed to grant. The proposition, then, that "Purchase breaks hire" holds in principle; for the full right in a thing as a property overbears all personal right, which is inconsistent with it. But there remains a right of action to the lessee, on the ground of a personal right for indemnification on account of any loss arising from breaking of the contract.

EPISODICAL SECTION. The Ideal Acquisition of External Objects of the Will.

32. The Nature and Modes of Ideal Acquisition.

I call that mode of acquisition ideal which involves no causality in time, and which is founded upon a mere idea of pure reason. It is nevertheless actual, and not merely imaginary acquisition: and it is not called real only because the act of acquisition is not empirical. This character of the act arises from the peculiarity that the person acquiring acquires from another who either is not yet, and who can only be regarded as a possible being, or who is just ceasing to be, or who no longer is. Hence such a mode of attaining to possession is to be regarded as a mere practical idea of reason.

There are three modes of ideal acquisition:

I. Acquisition by usucapion;

II. Acquisition by inheritance or succession;

III. Acquisition by undying merit (meritum immortale), or the claim by right to a good name at death.

These three modes of acquisition can, as a matter of fact, only have effect in a public juridical state of existence, but they are not founded merely upon the civil constitution or upon arbitrary statutes; they are already contained a priori in the conception of the state of nature, and are thus necessarily conceivable prior to their empirical manifestation. The laws regarding them in the civil constitution ought to be regulated by that rational conception.

33. I. Acquisition by Usucapion.

(Acquisitio per Usucapionem).

I may acquire the property of another merely by long possession and use of it (usucapio). Such property is not acquired, because I may legitimately presume that his consent is given to this effect (per consensum praesumptum); nor because I can assume that, as he does not oppose my acquisition of it, he has relinquished or abandoned it as his (rem derelictam). But I acquire it thus because, even if there were any one actually raising a claim to this property as its true owner, I may exclude him on the ground of my long possession of it, ignore his previous existence, and proceed as if he existed during the time of my possession as a mere abstraction, although I may have been subsequently apprized of his reality as well as of his claim. This mode of acquisition is not quite correctly designated acquisition by prescription (per praescriptionem); for the exclusion of all other claimants is to be regarded as only the consequence of the usucapion; and the process of acquisition must have gone before the right of exclusion. The rational possibility of such a mode of acquisition has now to be proved.

Any one who does not exercise a continuous possessory activity (actus possessorius) in relation to a thing as his is regarded with good right as one who does not at all exist as its possessor. For he cannot complain of lesion so long as he does not qualify himself with a title as its possessor. And even if he should afterwards lay claim to the thing when another has already taken possession of it, he only says he was once on a time owner of it, but not that he is so still, or that his possession has continued without interruption as a juridical fact. It can, therefore, only be a juridical process of possession, that has been maintained without interruption and is proveable by documentary fact, that any one can secure for himself what is his own after ceasing for a long time to make use of it.

For, suppose that the neglect to exercise this possessory activity had not the effect of enabling another to found upon his hitherto lawful, undisputed and bona fide possession, and irrefragable right to continue in its possession so that he may regard the thing that is thus in his possession as acquired by him. Then no acquisition would ever become peremptory and secured, but all acquisition would only be provisory and temporary. This is evident on the ground that there are no historical records available to carry the investigation of a title back to the first possessor and his act of acquisition. The presumption upon which acquisition by usucapion is founded is, therefore, not merely its conformity to right as allowed and just, but also the presumption of its being right (praesumtio juris et de jure), and its being assumed to be in accordance with compulsory laws (suppositio legalis). Anyone who has neglected to embody his possessory act in a documentary title has lost his claim to the right of being possessor for the time; and the length of the period of his neglecting to do so- which need not necessarily be particularly defined- can be referred to only as establishing the certainty of this neglect. And it would contradict the postulate of the juridically practical reason to maintain that one hitherto unknown as a possessor, and whose possessory activity has at least been interrupted, whether by or without fault of his own, could always at any time re-acquire a property; for this would be to make all ownership uncertain (dominia rerum incerta facere).

But if he is a member of the commonwealth or civil union, the state may maintain his possession for him vicariously, although it may be interrupted as private possession; and in that case the actual possessor will not be able to prove a title of acquisition even from a first occupation, nor to found upon a title of usucapion. But, in the state of nature, usucapion is universally a rightful ground of holding, not properly as a juridical mode of requiring a thing, but as a ground for maintaining oneself in possession of it where there are no juridical acts. A release from juridical claims is commonly also called acquisition. The prescriptive title of the older possessor, therefore, belongs to the sphere of natural right (est juris naturae).

34. II. Acquisition by Inheritance.

(Acquisitio haereditatis).

Inheritance is constituted by the transfer (translatio) of the property or goods of one who is dying to a survivor, through the consent of the will of both. The acquisition of the heir who takes the estate (haeredis instituti) and the relinquishment of the testator who leaves it, being the acts that constitute the exchange of the mine and thine, take place in the same moment of time- in articulo mortis- and just when the testator ceases to be. There is therefore no special act of transfer (translatio) in the empirical sense; for that would involve two successive acts, by which the one would first divest himself of his possession, and the other would thereupon enter into it. Inheritance as constituted by a simultaneous double act is, therefore, an ideal mode of acquisition. Inheritance is inconceivable in the state of nature without a testamentary disposition (dispositio ultimae voluntatis); and the question arises as to whether this mode of acquisition is to be regarded as a contract of succession, or a unilateral act instituting an heir by a will (testamentum). The determination of this question depends on the further question, whether and how, in the very same moment in which one individual ceases to be, there can be a transition of his property to another person. Hence the problem, as to how a mode of acquisition by inheritance is possible, must be investigated independently of the various possible forms in which it is practically carried out, and which can have place only in a commonwealth.

"It is possible to acquire by being instituted or appointed heir in a testamentary disposition." For the testator Caius promises and declares in his last will to Titius, who knows nothing of this promise, to transfer to him his estate in case of death, but thus continuing as long as he lives sole owner of it. Now by a mere unilateral act of will, nothing can in fact be transmitted to another person, as in addition to the promise of the one party there is required acceptance (acceptatio) on the part of the other, and a simultaneous bilateral act of will (voluntas simultanea) which, however, is here awanting. So long as Caius lives, Titius cannot expressly accept in order to enter on acquisition, because Caius has only promised in case of death; otherwise the property would be for a moment at least in common possession, which is not the will of the testator. However, Titius acquires tacitly a special right to the inheritance as a real right. This is constituted by the sole and exclusive right to accept the estate (jus in re jacente), which is therefore called at that point of time a haereditas jacens. Now as every man- because he must always gain and never lose by it- necessarily, although tacitly, accepts such a right, and as Titius after the death of Caius is in this position, he may acquire the succession as heir by acceptance of the promise. And the estate is not in the meantime entirely without an owner (res nullius), but is only in abeyance or vacant (vacua); because he has exclusively the right of choice as to whether he will actually make the estate bequeathed to him his own or not.

Hence testaments are valid according to mere natural right (sunt juris naturae). This assertion however, is to be understood in the sense that they are capable and worthy of being introduced and sanctioned in the civil state, whenever it is instituted. For it is only the common will in the civil state that maintains the possession of the inheritance or succession, while it hangs between acceptance or rejection and specially belongs to no particular individual.

35. III. The Continuing Right of a Good Name

after Death. (Bona fama Defuncti).

It would be absurd to think that a dead person could possess anything after his death, when he no longer exists in the eye of the law, if the matter in question were a mere thing. But a good name is a congenital and external, although merely ideal, possession, which attaches inseparably to the individual as a person. Now we can and must abstract here from all consideration as to whether the persons cease to be after death or still continue as such to exist; because, in considering their juridical relation to others, we regard persons merely according to their humanity and as rational beings (homo noumenon). Hence any attempt to bring the reputation or good name of a person into evil and false repute after death, is always questionable, even although a well-founded charge may be allowed- for to that extent the brocard "De mortuis nil nisi bene"* is wrong. Yet to spread charges against one who is absent and cannot defend himself, shows at least a want of magnanimity.

*[Let nothing be said of the dead but what is favourable.]

By a blameless life and a death that worthily ends it, nothing ends it, it is admitted that a man may acquire a (negatively) good reputation constituting something that is his own, even when he no longer exists in the world of sense as a visible person (homo phaenomenon). It is further held that his survivors and successors- whether relatives or strangers- are entitled to defend his good name as a matter of right, on the ground that unproved accusations subject them all to the danger of similar treatment after death. Now that a man when dead can yet acquire such a right is a peculiar and, nevertheless, an undeniable manifestation in fact, of the a priori law-giving reason thus extending its law of command or prohibition beyond the limits of the present life. If some one then spreads a charge regarding a dead person that would have dishonoured him when living, or even made him despicable, any one who can adduce a proof that this accusation is intentionally false and untrue may publicly declare him who thus brings the dead person into ill repute to be a calumniator, and affix dishonour to him in turn. This would not be allowable unless it were legitimate to assume that the dead person was injured by the accusation, although he is dead, and that a certain just satisfaction was done to him by an apology, although he no longer sensibly exists. A title to act the part the vindicator of the dead person does not require to be established; for every one necessarily claims this of himself, not merely as a duty of virtue regarded ethically, but as a right belonging to him in virtue of his humanity. Nor does the vindicator require to show any special personal damage, accruing to him as a friend or relative, from a stain on the character of the deceased, to justify him in proceeding to censure it. That such a form of ideal acquisition, and even a right in an individual after death against survivors, is thus actually founded, cannot, therefore, be disputed, although the possibility of such a right is not capable of logical deduction.

There is no ground for drawing visionary inferences from what has just been stated, to the presentiment of a future life and invisible relations to departed souls. For the considerations connected with this right turn on nothing more than the purely moral and juridical relation which subsists among men, even in the present life, as rational beings. Abstraction is, however, made from all that belongs physically to their existence in space and time; that is, men are considered logically apart from these physical concomitants of their nature, not as to their state when actually deprived of them, but only in so far as being spirits they are in a condition that might realize the injury done them by calumniators. Any one who may falsely say something against me a hundred years hence injures me even now. For in the pure juridical relation, which is entirely rational and surprasensible, abstraction is made from the physical conditions of time, and the calumniator is as culpable as if he had committed the offence in my lifetime; only this will not be tried by a criminal process, but he will only be punished with that loss of honour he would have caused to another, and this is inflicted upon him by public opinion according to the lex talionis. Even a plagiarism from a dead author, although it does not tarnish the honour of the deceased, but only deprives him of a part of his property, is yet properly regarded as a lesion of his human right.

FIRST PART. PRIVATE RIGHT.
The System of those Laws Which Require No External Promulgation.
CHAPTER III. Acquisition Conditioned by the Sentence of
a Public Judicatory.
36. How and What Acquisition is Subjectively Conditioned
by the Principle of a Public Court.

Natural right, understood simply as that right which is not statutory, and which is knowable purely a priori, by every man's reason, will include distributive justice as well as commutative justice. It is manifest that the latter, as constituting the justice that is valid between persons in their reciprocal relations of intercourse with one another, must belong to natural right. But this holds also of distributive justice, in so far as it can be known a priori; and decisions or sentences regarding it must be regulated by the law of natural right.

The moral person who presides in the sphere of justice and administers it is called the Court of justice, and, as engaged in the process of official duty, the judicatory; the sentence delivered in a case, is the judgement (judicium). All this is to be here viewed a priori, according to the rational conditions of right, without taking into consideration how such a constitution is to be actually established or organized, for which particular statutes, and consequently empirical principles, are requisite.

The question, then, in this connection, is not merely "What is right in itself?" in the sense in which every man must determine it by the judgement of reason; but "What is right as applied to this case?" that is, "What is right and just as viewed by a court?" The rational and the judicial points of view are therefore to be distinguished; and there are four cases in which the two forms of judgement have a different and opposite issue. And yet they may co-exist with each other, because they are delivered from two different, yet respectively true, points of view: the one from regard to private right, the other from the idea of public right. They are: I. The contract of donation (pactum donationis); II. The contract of loan (commodatum); III. The action of real revindication (vindicatio); and IV. Guarantee by oath (juramentum).

It is a common error on the part of the jurist to fall here into the fallacy of begging the question by a tacit assumption (vitium subreptionis). This is done by assuming as objective and absolute the juridical principle which a public court of justice is entitled and even bound to adopt in its own behoof, and only from the subjective purpose of qualifying itself to decide and judge upon all the rights pertaining to individuals. It is therefore of no small importance to make this specific difference intelligible, and to draw attention to it.

37. I. The Contract of Donation.

(Pactum Donationis).

The contract of donation signifies the gratuitous alienation (gratis) of a thing or right that is mine. It involves a relation between me as the donor (donans), and another person as the donatory (donatarius), in accordance with the principle of private right, by which what is mine is transferred to the latter, on his acceptance of it, as a gift (donum). However, it is not to be presumed that I have voluntarily bound myself thereby so as to be compelled to keep my promise, and that I have thus given away my freedom gratuitously, and, as it were, to that extent thrown myself away. Nemo suum jactare praesumitur. But this is what would happen, under such circumstances, according to the principle of right in the civil state; for in this sphere the donatory can compel me, under certain conditions, to perform my promise. If, then, the case comes before a court, according to the conditions of public right, it must either be presumed that the donor has consented to such compulsion, or the court would give no regard, in the sentence, to the consideration as to whether he intended to reserve the right to resile from his promise or not; but would only refer to what is certain, namely, the condition of the promise and the acceptance of the donatory. Although the promiser, therefore, thought- as may easily be supposed- that he could not be bound by his promise in any case, if he "rued" it before it was actually carried out, yet the court assumes that he ought expressly to have reserved this condition if such was his mind; and if he did not make such an express reservation, it will be held that he can be compelled to implement his promise. And this principle is assumed by the court, because the administration of justice would otherwise be endlessly impeded, or even made entirely impossible.

38. II. The Contract of Loan. (Commodatum).

In the contract of commodate-loan (commodatum) I give some one the gratuitous use of something that is mine. If it is a thing that is given on loan, the contracting parties agree that the borrower will restore the very same thing to the power of the lender, But the receiver of the loan (commodatarius) cannot, at the same time, assume that the owner of the thing lent (commodans) will take upon himself all risk (casus) of any possible loss of it, or of its useful quality, that may arise from having given it into the possession of the receiver. For it is not to be understood of itself that the owner, besides the use of the thing, which he has granted to the receiver, and the detriment that is inseparable from such use, also gives a guarantee or warrandice against all damage that may arise from such use. On the contrary, a special accessory contract would have to be entered into for this purpose. The only question, then, that can be raised is this: "Is it incumbent on the lender or the borrower to add expressly the condition of undertaking the risk that may accrue to the thing lent; or, if this is not done, which of the parties is to be presumed to have consented and agreed to guarantee the property of the lender, up to restoration of the very same thing or its equivalent?" Certainly not the lender; because it cannot be presumed that he has gratuitously agreed to give more than the mere use of the thing, so that he cannot be supposed to have also undertaken the risk of loss of his property. But this may be assumed on the side of the borrower; because he thereby undertakes and performs nothing more than what is implied in the contract.

For example, I enter a house, when overtaken by a shower of rain, and ask the loan of a cloak. But through accidental contact with colouring matter, it becomes entirely spoiled while in my possession; or on entering another house, I lay it aside and it is stolen. Under such circumstances, everybody would think it absurd for me to assert that I had no further concern with the cloak but to return it as it was, or, in the latter case, only to mention the fact of the theft; and that, in any case, anything more required would be but an act of courtesy in expressing sympathy with the owner on account of his loss, seeing he can claim nothing on the ground of right. It would be otherwise, however, if, on asking the use of an article, I discharged myself beforehand from all responsibility, in case of its coming to grief while in my hands, on the ground of my being poor and unable to compensate any incidental loss. No one could find such a condition superfluous or ludicrous, unless the borrower were, in fact, known to be a well-to-do and well-disposed man; because in such a case it would almost be an insult not to act on the presumption of generous compensation for any loss sustained.

Now by the very nature of this contract, the possible damage (casus) which the thing lent may undergo cannot be exactly determined in any agreement. Commodate is therefore an uncertain contract (pactum incertum), because the consent can only be so far presumed. The judgement, in any case, deciding upon whom the incidence of any loss must fall, cannot therefore be determined from the conditions of the contract in itself, but only by the principle of the court before which it comes, and which can only consider what is certain in the contract; and the only thing certain is always the fact as to the possession of the thing as property. Hence the judgement passed in the state of nature will be different from that given by a court of justice in the civil state. The judgement from the standpoint of natural right will be determined by regard to the inner rational quality of the thing, and will run thus: "Loss arising from damage accruing to a thing lent falls upon the borrower" (casum sentit commodatarius); whereas the sentence of a court of justice in the civil state will run thus: "The loss falls upon the lender" (casum sentit dominus). The latter judgement turns out differently from the former as the sentence of the mere sound reason, because a public judge cannot found upon presumptions as to what either party may have thought; and thus the one who has not obtained release from all loss in the thing, by a special accessory contract, must bear the loss. Hence the difference between the judgement as the court must deliver it and the form in which each individual is entitled to hold it for himself, by his private reason, is a matter of importance, and is not to be overlooked in the consideration of juridical judgements.

39. III. The Revindication of what has been Lost.

(Vindicatio).

It is clear from what has been already said that a thing of mine which continues to exist remains mine, although I may not be in continuous occupation of it; and that it does not cease to be mine without a juridical act of dereliction or alienation. Further, it is evident that a right in this thing (jus reale) belongs in consequence to me (jus personale), against every holder of it, and not merely against some particular person. But the question now arises as to whether this right must be regarded by every other person as a continuous right of property per se, if I have not in any way renounced it, although the thing is in the possession of another.

A thing may be lost (res amissa) and thus come into other hands in an honourable bona fide way as a supposed "find"; or it may come to me by formal transfer on the part of one who is in possession of it, and who professes to be its owner, although he is not so. Taking the latter case, the question arises whether, since I cannot acquire a thing from one who is not its owner (a non domino), I am excluded by the fact from all right in the thing itself, and have merely a personal right against a wrongful possessor? This is manifestly so, if the acquisition is judged purely according to its inner justifying grounds and viewed according to the state of nature, and not according to the convenience of a court of justice.

For everything alienable must be capable of being acquired by anyone. The rightfulness of acquisition, however, rests entirely upon the form in accordance with which what is in possession of another, is transferred to me and accepted by me. In other words, rightful acquisition depends upon the formality of the juridical act of commutation or interchange between the possessor of the thing and the acquirer of it, without its being required to ask how the former came by it; because this would itself be an injury, on the ground that: Quilibet praesumitur bonus. Now suppose it turned out that the said possessor was not the real owner, I cannot admit that the real owner is entitled to hold me directly responsible, or so entitled with regard to any one who might be holding the thing. For I have myself taken nothing away from him, when, for example, I bought his horse according to the law (titulo empti venditi) when it was offered for sale in the public market. The title of acquisition is therefore unimpeachable on my side; and as buyer I am not bound, nor even have I the right, to investigate the title of the seller; for this process of investigation would have to go on in an ascending series ad infinitum. Hence on such grounds I ought to be regarded, in virtue of a regular and formal purchase, as not merely the putative, but the real owner of the horse.

But against this position, there immediately start up the following juridical principles. Any acquisition derived from one who is not the owner of the thing in question is null and void. I cannot derive from another anything more than what he himself rightfully has; and although as regards the form of the acquisition the modus acquirendi- I may proceed in accordance with all the conditions of right when I deal in a stolen horse exposed for sale in the market, yet a real title warranting the acquisition was awanting; for the horse was not really the property of the seller in question. However I may be a bona fide possessor of a thing under such conditions, I am still only a putative owner, and the real owner has the right of vindication against me (rem suam vindicandi).

Now, it may be again asked, what is right and just in itself regarding the acquisition of external things among men in their intercourse with one another- viewed in the state of nature according to the principles of commutative justice? And it must be admitted in this connection that whoever has a purpose of acquiring anything must regard it as absolutely necessary to investigate whether the thing which he wishes to acquire does not already belong to another person. For although he may carefully observe the formal conditions required for appropriating what may belong to the property of another, as in buying a horse according to the usual terms in a market, yet he can, at the most, acquire only a personal right in relation to a thing (jus ad rem) so long as it is still unknown to him whether another than the seller may not be the real owner. Hence, if some other person were to come forward and prove by documentary evidence a prior right of property in the thing, nothing would remain for the putative new owner but the advantage which he has drawn as a bona fide possessor of it up to that moment. Now it is frequently impossible to discover the absolutely first original owner of a thing in the series of putative owners, who derive their right from one another. Hence no mere exchange of external things, however well it may agree with the formal conditions of commutative justice, can ever guarantee an absolutely certain acquisition.

Here, however, the juridically law-giving reason comes in again with the principle of distributive justice; and it adopts as a criterion of the rightfulness of possession, not what is in itself in reference to the private will of each individual in the state of nature, but only the consideration of how it would be adjudged by a court of justice in a civil state, constituted by the united will of all. In this connection, fulfillment of the formal conditions of acquisition, that in themselves only establish a personal right, is postulated as sufficient; and they stand as an equivalent for the material conditions which properly establish the derivation of property from a prior putative owner, to the extent of making what is in itself only a personal right, valid before a court, as a real right. Thus the horse which I bought when exposed for sale in the public market, under conditions regulated by the municipal law, becomes my property if all the conditions of purchase and sale have been exactly observed in the transaction; but always under the reservation that the real owner continues to have the right of a claim against the seller, on the ground of his prior unalienated possession. My otherwise personal right is thus transmuted into a real right, according to which I may take and vindicate the object as mine wherever I may find it, without being responsible for the way in which the Seller had come into possession of it.

It is therefore only in behoof of the requirements of juridical decision in a court (in favorem justitiae distributivae) that the right in respect of a thing is regarded, not as personal, which it is in itself, but as real, because it can thus be most easily and certainly adjudged; and it is thus accepted and dealt with according to a pure principle a priori. Upon this principle, various statutory laws come to be founded which specially aim at laying down the conditions under which alone a mode of acquisition shall be legitimate, so that the judge may be able to assign every one his own as easily and certainly as possible. Thus, in the brocard, "Purchase breaks hire," what by the nature of the subject is a real right- namely the hire- is taken to hold as a merely personal right; and, conversely, as in the case referred to above, what is in itself merely a personal right is held to be valid as a real right. And this is done only when the question arises as to the principles by which a court of justice in the civil state is to be guided, in order to proceed with all possible safety in delivering judgement on the rights of individuals.

40. IV. Acquisition of Security by the Taking of an Oath.

(Cautio Juratoria).

Only one ground can be assigned on which it could be held that men are bound in the juridical relation to believe and to confess that there are gods, or that there is a God. It is that they may be able to swear an oath; and that thus by the fear of an all-seeing Supreme Power, whose revenge they must solemnly invoke upon themselves in case their utterance should be false, they may be constrained to be truthful in statement and faithful in promising. It is not morality but merely blind superstition that is reckoned upon in this process; for it is evident it implies that no certainty is to be expected from a mere solemn declaration in matters of right before a court, although the duty of truthfulness must have always appeared self-evident to all, in a matter which concerns the holiest that can be among men- namely, the right of man. Hence recourse has been had to a motive founded on mere myths and fables as imaginary guarantees. Thus among the Rejangs, a heathen people in Sumatra, it is the custom- according to the testimony of Marsden- to swear by the bones of their dead relatives, although they have no belief in a life after death. In like manner the negroes of Guinea swear by their fetish, a bird's feather, which they imprecate under the belief that it will break their neck. And so in other cases. The belief underlying these oaths is that an invisible power- whether it has understanding or not- by its very nature possesses magical power that can be put into action by such invocations. Such a belief- which is commonly called religion, but which ought to be called superstition- is, however, indispensable for the administration of justice; because, without referring to it, a court of justice would not have adequate means to ascertain facts otherwise kept secret, and to determine rights. A law making an oath obligatory is therefore only given in behoof of the judicial authority.

But then the question arises as to what the obligation could be founded upon that would bind any one in a court of justice to accept the oath of another person as a right and valid proof of the truth of his statements which are to put an end to all dispute. In other words, what obliges me juridically to believe that another person when taking an oath has any religion at all, so that I should subordinate or entrust my right to his oath? And, on like grounds, conversely, can I be bound at all to take an oath? It is evident that both these questions point to what is in itself morally wrong.

But in relation to a court of justice- and generally in the civil state- if it be assumed there are no other means of getting to the truth in certain cases than by an oath, it must be adopted. In regard to religion, under the supposition that every one has it, it may be utilized as a necessary means (in causu necessitatis), in behoof of the legitimate procedure of a court of justice. The court uses this form of spiritual compulsion (tortura spiritualis) as an available means, in conformity with the superstitious propensity of mankind, for the ascertainment of what is concealed; and therefore holds itself justified in so doing. The legislative power, however, is fundamentally wrong in assigning this authority to the judicial power, because even in the civil state any compulsion with regard to the taking of oaths is contrary to the inalienable freedom of man.

Official oaths, which are usually promissory, being taken on entering upon an office, to the effect that the individual has sincere intention to administer his functions dutifully, might well be changed into assertory oaths, to be taken at the end of a year or more of actual administration, the official swearing to the faithfulness of his discharge of duty during that time. This would bring the conscience more into action than the promissory oath, which always gives room for the internal pretext that, with the best intention, the difficulties that arose during the administration of the official function were not foreseen. And, further, violations of duty, under the prospect of their being summed up by future censors, would give rise to more anxiety as to censure than when they are merely represented, one after the other, and forgotten.

As regards an oath taken concerning a matter of belief (de credulitate), it is evident that no such oath can be demanded by a court. 1. For, first, it contains in itself a contradiction. Such belief, as intermediate between opinion and knowledge, is a thing on which one might venture to lay a wager but not to swear an oath. 2. And, second, the judge who imposes an oath of belief, in order to ascertain anything pertinent to his own purpose or even to the common good, commits a great offence against the conscientiousness of the party taking such an oath. This he does in regard both to the levity of mind, which he thereby helps to engender, and to the stings of conscience which a man must feel who to-day regards a subject from a certain point of view, but who will very probably to-morrow find it quite improbable from another point of view. Any one, therefore, who is compelled to take such an oath, is subjected to an injury.

Transition from the Mine and Thine in the State of Nature to the Mine and Thine in the Juridical State Generally.

41. Public Justice as Related to the Natural and the Civil State.

The juridical state is that relation of men to one another which contains the conditions under which it is alone possible for every one to obtain the right that is his due. The formal principle of the possibility of actually participating in such right, viewed in accordance with the idea of a universally legislative will, is public justice. Public justice may be considered in relation either to the possibility, or actuality, or necessity of the possession of objects- regarded as the matter of the activity of the will- according to laws. It may thus be divided into protective justice (justitia testatrix), commutative justice (justitia commutativa), and distributive justice (justitia distributiva), in the first mode of justice, the law declares merely what relation is internally right in respect of form (lex justi); in the second, it declares what is likewise externally in accord with a law in respect of the object, and what possession is rightful (lex juridica); and in the third, it declares what is right, and what is just, and to what extent, by the judgement of a court in any particular case coming under the given law. In this latter relation, the public court is called the justice of the country; and the question whether there actually is or is not such an administration of public justice may be regarded as the most important of all juridical interests.

The non-juridical state is that condition of society in which there is no distributive justice. It is commonly called the natural state (status naturalis), or the state of nature. It is not the social state, as Achenwall puts it, for this may be in itself an artificial state (status artificialis), that is to be contradistinguished from the "natural" state. The opposite of the state of nature is the civil state (status civilis) as the condition of a society standing under a distributive justice. In the state of nature, there may even be juridical forms of society such as marriage, parental authority, the household, and such like. For none of these, however, does any law a priori lay it down as an incumbent obligation: "Thou shalt enter into this state." But it may be said of the juridical state that: "All men who may even involuntarily come into relations of right with one another ought to enter into this state."

The natural or non-juridical social state may be viewed as the sphere of private right, and the civil state may be specially regarded as the sphere of public right. The latter state contains no more and no other duties of men towards each other than what may be conceived in connection with the former state; the matter of private right is, in short, the very same in both. The laws of the civil state, therefore, only turn upon the juridical form of the coexistence of men under a common constitution; and, in this respect, these laws must necessarily be regarded and conceived as public laws.

The civil union (unio civilis) cannot, in the strict sense, be properly called a society; for there is no sociality in common between the ruler (imperans) and the subject (subditus) under a civil constitution. They are not co-ordinated as associates in a society with each other, but the one is subordinated to the other. Those who may be co-ordinated with one another must consider themselves as mutually equal, in so far as they stand under common laws. The civil union may therefore be regarded not so much as being, but rather as making a society.

42. The Postulate of Public Right.

From the conditions of private right in the natural state, there arises the postulate of public right. It may be thus expressed: "In the relation of unavoidable coexistence with others, thou shalt pass from the state of nature into a juridical union constituted under the condition of a distributive justice." The principle of this postulate may be unfolded analytically from the conception of right in the external relation, contradistinguished from mere might as violence.

No one is under obligation to abstain from interfering with the possession of others, unless they give him a reciprocal guarantee for the observance of a similar abstention from interference with his possession. Nor does he require to wait for proof by experience of the need of this guarantee, in view of the antagonistic disposition of others. He is therefore under no obligation to wait till he acquires practical prudence at his own cost; for he can perceive in himself evidence of the natural inclination of men to play the master over others, and to disregard the claims of the right of others, when they feel themselves their superiors by might or fraud. And thus it is not necessary to wait for the melancholy experience of actual hostility; the individual is from the first entitled to exercise a rightful compulsion towards those who already threaten him by their very nature. Quilibet praesumitur malus, donec securitatem dederit oppositi.

So long as the intention to live and continue in this state of externally lawless freedom prevails, men may be said to do no wrong or injustice at all to one another, even when they wage war against each other. For what seems competent as good for the one is equally valid for the other, as if it were so by mutual agreement. Uti partes de jure suo disponunt, ita jus est. But generally they must be considered as being in the highest state of wrong, as being and willing to be in a condition which is not juridical, and in which, therefore, no one can be secured against violence, in the possession of his own.

The distinction between what is only formally and what is also materially wrong, and unjust, finds frequent application in the science of right. An enemy who, on occupying a besieged fortress, instead of honourably fulfilling the conditions of a capitulation, maltreats the garrison on marching out, or otherwise violates the agreement, cannot complain of injury or wrong if on another occasion the same treatment is inflicted upon themselves. But, in fact, all such actions fundamentally involve the commission of wrong and injustice, in the highest degree; because they take all validity away from the conception of right, and give up everything, as it were by law itself, to savage violence, and thus overthrow the rights of men generally.

SECOND PART. PUBLIC RIGHT.
THE SYSTEM OF THOSE LAWS WHICH REQUIRE PUBLIC PROMULGATION.
THE PRINCIPLES OF RIGHT IN CIVIL SOCIETY.
43. Definition and Division of Public Right.

Public right embraces the whole of the laws that require to be universally promulgated in order to produce juridical state of society. It is therefore a system of those laws that are requisite for a people as a multitude of men forming a nation, or for a number of nations, in their relations to each other. Men and nations, on account of their mutual influence on one another, require a juridical constitution uniting them under one will, in order that they may participate in what is right. This relation of the individuals of a nation to each other constitutes the civil union in the social state; and, viewed as a whole in relation to its constituent members, it forms the political state (civitas).

1. The state, as constituted by the common interest of all to live in a juridical union, is called, in view of its form, the commonwealth or the republic in the wider sense of the term (res publica latius sic dicta). The principles of right in this sphere thus constitute the first department of public right as the right of the state (jus civitatis) or national right. 2. The state, again, viewed in relation to other peoples, is called a power (potentia), whence arises the idea of potentates. Viewed in relation to the supposed hereditary unity of the people composing it, the state constitutes a nation (gens). Under the general conception of public right, in addition to the right of the individual state, there thus arises another department of right, constituting the right of nations (jus gentium) or international right. 3. Further, as the surface of the earth is not unlimited in extent, but is circumscribed into a unity, national right and international right necessarily culminate in the idea of a universal right of mankind, which may be called Cosmopolitical Right (jus cosmopoliticum). And national, international, and cosmopolitical right are so interconnected, that, if any one of these three possible forms of the juridical relation fails to embody the essential principles that ought to regulate external freedom by law, the structure of legislation reared by the others will also be undermined, and the whole system would

at last fall to pieces.

I. Right of the State and Constitutional Law.

(Jus Civitatis).

44. Origin Of the Civil Union and Public Right.

It is not from any experience prior to the appearance of an external authoritative legislation that we learn of the maxim of natural violence among men and their evil tendency to engage in war with each other. Nor is it assumed here that it is merely some particular historical condition or fact, that makes public legislative constraint necessary; for however well-disposed or favourable to right men may be considered to be of themselves, the rational idea of a state of society not yet regulated by right, must be taken as our starting-point. This idea implies that before a legal state of society can be publicly established, individual men, nations, and states, can never be safe against violence from each other; and this is evident from the consideration that every one of his own will naturally does what seems good and right in his own eyes, entirely independent of the opinion of others. Hence, unless the institution of right is to be renounced, the first thing incumbent on men is to accept the principle that it is necessary to leave the state of nature, in which every one follows his own inclinations, and to form a union of all those who cannot avoid coming into reciprocal communication, and thus subject themselves in common to the external restraint of public compulsory laws. Men thus enter into a civil union, in which every one has it determined by law what shall be recognized as his; and this is secured to him by a competent external power distinct from his own individuality. Such is the primary obligation, on the part of all men, to enter into the relations of a civil state of society.

The natural condition of mankind need not, on this ground, be represented as a state of absolute injustice, as if there could have been no other relation originally among men but what was merely determined by force. But this natural condition must be regarded, if it ever existed, as a state of society that was void of regulation by right (status justitiae vacuus), so that if a matter of right came to be in dispute (jus controversum), no competent judge was found to give an authorized legal decision upon it. It is therefore reasonable that any one should constrain another by force, to pass from such a nonjuridical state of life and enter within the jurisdiction of a civil state of society. For, although on the basis of the ideas of right held by individuals as such, external things may be acquired by occupancy or contract, yet such acquisition is only provisory so long as it has not yet obtained the sanction of a public law. Till this sanction is reached, the condition of possession is not determined by any public distributive justice, nor is it secured by any power exercising public right.

If men were not disposed to recognize any acquisition at all as rightful- even in a provisional way- prior to entering into the civil state, this state of society would itself be impossible. For the laws regarding the mine and thine in the state of nature, contain formally the very same thing as they prescribe in the civil state, when it is viewed merely according to rational conceptions: only that in the forms of the civil state the conditions are laid down under which the formal prescriptions of the state of nature attain realization conformable to distributive justice. Were there, then, not even provisionally, an external meum and tuum in the state of nature, neither would there be any juridical duties in relation to them; and, consequently, there would be no obligation to pass out of that state into another.

45. The Form of the State and its Three Powers.

A state (civitas) is the union of a number of men under juridical laws. These laws, as such, are to be regarded as necessary a priori- that is, as following of themselves from the conceptions of external right generally- and not as merely established by statute. The form of the state is thus involved in the idea of the state, viewed as it ought to be according to pure principles of right; and this ideal form furnishes the normal criterion of every real union that constitutes a commonwealth.

Every state contains in itself three powers, the universal united will of the people being thus personified in a political triad. These are the legislative power, the executive power, and the judiciary power. 1. The legislative power of the sovereignty in the state is embodied in the person of the lawgiver; 2. the executive power is embodied in the person of the ruler who administers the Law; and 3. the judiciary power, embodied in the person of the judge, is the function of assigning every one what is his own, according to the law (potestas legislatoria, rectoria, et judiciaria). These three powers may be compared to the three propositions in a practical syllogism: the major as the sumption laying down the universal law of a will, the minor presenting the command applicable to an action according to the law as the principle of the subsumption, and the conclusion containing the sentence, or judgement of right, in the particular case under consideration.

46. The Legislative Power and the Members of the State.

The legislative power, viewed in its rational principle, can only belong to the united will of the people. For, as all right ought to proceed from this power, it is necessary that its laws should be unable to do wrong to any one whatever. Now, if any one individual determines anything in the state in contradistinction to another, it is always possible that he may perpetrate a wrong on that other; but this is never possible when all determine and decree what is to be Law to themselves. Volenti non fit injuria. Hence it is only the united and consenting will of all the people- in so far as each of them determines the same thing about all, and all determine the same thing about each- that ought to have the power of enacting law in the state.

The members of a civil society thus united for the purpose of legislation, and thereby constituting a state, are called its citizens; and there are three juridical attributes that inseparably belong to them by right. These are: 1. constitutional freedom, as the right of every citizen to have to obey no other law than that to which he has given his consent or approval; 2. civil equality, as the right of the citizen to recognise no one as a superior among the people in relation to himself, except in so far as such a one is as subject to his moral power to impose obligations, as that other has power to impose obligations upon him; and 3. political independence, as the light to owe his existence and continuance in society not to the arbitrary will of another, but to his own rights and powers as a member of the commonwealth, and, consequently, the possession of a civil personality, which cannot be represented by any other than himself.

The capability of voting by possession of the suffrage properly constitutes the political qualification of a citizen as a member of the state. But this, again, presupposes the independence or self-sufficiency of the individual citizen among the people, as one who is not a mere incidental part of the commonwealth, but a member of it acting of his own will in community with others. The last of the three qualities involved necessarily constitutes the distinction between active and passive citizenship; although the latter conception appears to stand in contradiction to the definition of a citizen as such. The following examples may serve to remove this difficulty. The apprentice of a merchant or tradesman, a servant who is not in the employ of the state, a minor (naturaliter vel civiliter), all women, and, generally, every one who is compelled to maintain himself not according to his own industry, but as it is arranged by others (the state excepted), are without civil personality, and their existence is only, as it were, incidentally included in the state. The woodcutter whom I employ on my estate; the smith in India who carries his hammer, anvil, and bellows into the houses where he is engaged to work in iron, as distinguished from the European carpenter or smith, who can offer the independent products of his labour as wares for public sale; the resident tutor as distinguished from the schoolmaster; the ploughman as distinguished from the farmer and such like, illustrate the distinction in question. In all these cases, the former members of the contrast are distinguished from the latter by being mere subsidiaries of the commonwealth and not active independent members of it, because they are of necessity commanded and protected by others, and consequently possess no political self-sufficiency in themselves. Such dependence on the will of others and the consequent inequality are, however, not inconsistent with the freedom and equality of the individuals as men helping to constitute the people. Much rather is it the case that it is only under such conditions that a people can become a state and enter into a civil constitution. But all are not equally qualified to exercise the right of suffrage under the constitution, and to be full citizens of the state, and not mere passive subjects under its protection. For, although they are entitled to demand to be treated by all the other citizens according to laws of natural freedom and equality, as passive parts of the state, it does not follow that they ought themselves to have the right to deal with the state as active members of it, to reorganize it, or to take action by way of introducing certain laws. All they have a right in their circumstances to claim may be no more than that whatever be the mode in which the positive laws are enacted, these laws must not be contrary to the natural laws that demand the freedom of all the people and the equality that is conformable thereto; and it must therefore be made possible for them to raise themselves from this passive condition in the state to the condition of active citizenship.

47. Dignities in the State and the Original Contract.

All these three powers in the state are dignities; and, as necessarily arising out of the idea of the state and essential generally to the foundation of its constitution, they are to be regarded as political dignities. They imply the relation between a universal sovereign as head of the state- which according to the laws of freedom can be none other than the people itself united into a nation- and the mass of the individuals of the nation as subjects. The former member of the relation is the ruling power, whose function is to govern (imperans); the latter is the ruled constituents of the state, whose function is to obey (subditi).

The act by which a people is represented as constituting itself into a state, is termed the original contract. This is properly only an outward mode of representing the idea by which the rightfulness of the process of organizing the constitution may be made conceivable. According to this representation, all and each of the people give up their external freedom in order to receive it immediately again as members of a commonwealth. The commonwealth is the people viewed as united altogether into a state. And thus it is not to be said that the individual in the state has sacrificed a part of his inborn external freedom for a particular purpose; but he has abandoned his wild lawless freedom wholly, in order to find all his proper freedom again entire and undiminished, but in the form of a regulated order of dependence, that is, in a civil state regulated by laws of right. This relation of dependence thus arises out of his own regulative law giving will.

48. Mutual Relations and Characteristics of the
Three Powers.

The three powers in the state, as regards their relations to each other, are, therefore: (1) coordinate with one another as so many moral persons, and the one is thus the complement of the other in the way of completing the constitution of the state; (2) they are likewise subordinate to one another, so that the one cannot at the same time usurp the function of the other by whose side it moves, each having its own principle and maintaining its authority in a particular person, but under the condition of the will of a superior; and further, (3) by the union of both these relations, they assign distributively to every subject in the state his own rights.

Considered as to their respective dignity, the three powers may be thus described. The will of the sovereign legislator, in respect of what constitutes the external mine and thine, is to be regarded as irreprehensible; the executive function of the supreme ruler is to be regarded as irresistible; and the judicial sentence of the supreme judge is to be regarded as irreversible, being beyond appeal.

49. Distinct Functions of the Three Powers.

Autonomy of the State

1. The executive power belongs to the governor or regent of the state, whether it assumes the form of a moral or individual person, as the king or prince (rex, princeps). This executive authority, as the supreme agent of the state, appoints the magistrates, and prescribes the rules to the people, in accordance with which individuals may acquire anything or maintain what is their own conformably to the law, each case being brought under its application. Regarded as a moral person, this executive authority constitutes the government. The orders issued by the government to the people and the magistrates, as well as to the higher ministerial administrators of the state (gubernatio), are rescripts or decrees, and not laws; for they terminate in the decision of particular cases, and are given forth as unchangeable. A government acting as an executive, and at the same time laying down the law as the legislative power, would be a despotic government, and would have to be contradistinguished from a patriotic government. A patriotic government, again, is to be distinguished from a paternal government (regimen paternale) which is the most despotic government of all, the citizens being dealt with by it as mere children. A patriotic government, however, is one in which the state, while dealing with the subjects as if they were members of a family, still treats them likewise as citizens, and according to laws that recognize their independence, each individual possessing himself and not being dependent on the absolute will of another beside him or above him.

2. The legislative authority ought not at the same time to be the executive or governor; for the governor, as administrator, should stand under the authority of the law, and is bound by it under the supreme control of the legislator. The legislative authority may therefore deprive the governor of his power, depose him, or reform his administration, but not punish him. This is the proper and only meaning of the common saying in England, "The King- as the supreme executive power- can do no wrong." For any such application of punishment would necessarily be an act of that very executive power to which the supreme right to compel according to law pertains, and which would itself be thus subjected to coercion; which is self-contradictory.

3. Further, neither the legislative power nor the executive power ought to exercise the judicial function, but only appoint judges as magistrates. It is the people who ought to judge themselves, through those of the citizens who are elected by free choice as their representatives for this purpose, and even specially for every process or cause. For the judicial sentence is a special act of public distributive justice performed by a judge or court as a constitutional administrator of the law, to a subject as one of the people. Such an act is not invested inherently with the power to determine and assign to any one what is his. Every individual among the people being merely passive in this relation to the supreme power, either the executive or the legislative authority might do him wrong in their determinations in cases of dispute regarding the property of individuals. It would not be the people themselves who thus determined, or who pronounced the judgements of "guilty" or "not guilty" regarding their fellow-citizens. For it is to the determination of this issue in a cause that the court has to apply the law; and it is by means of the executive authority, that the judge holds power to assign to every one his own. Hence it is only the people that properly can judge in a cause- although indirectly representatives elected and deputed by themselves, as in a jury. It would even be beneath the dignity of the sovereign head of the state to play the judge; for this would be to put himself into a position in which it would be possible to do wrong, and thus to subject himself to the demand for an appeal to a still higher power (a rege male informato ad regem melius informandum).

It is by the co-operation of these three powers- the legislative, the executive, and the judicial- that the state realizes its autonomy. This autonomy consists in its organizing, forming, and maintaining itself in accordance with the laws of freedom. In their union the welfare of the state is realized. Salus reipublicae suprema lex.* By this is not to be understood merely the individual well-being and happiness of the citizens of the state; for- as Rousseau asserts- this end may perhaps be more agreeably and more desirably attained in the state of nature, or even under a despotic government. But the welfare of the state, as its own highest good, signifies that condition in which the greatest harmony is attained between its constitution and the principles of right- a condition of the state which reason by a categorical imperative makes it obligatory upon us to strive after.

*["The health of the state is the highest law."]

Constitutional and Juridical Consequences arising from
the Nature of the Civil Union.

A. Right of the Supreme Power; Treason; Dethronement;
Revolution; Reform.

The origin of the supreme power is practically inscrutable by the people who are placed under its authority. In other words, the subject need not reason too curiously in regard to its origin in the practical relation, as if the right of the obedience due to it were to be doubted (jus controversum). For as the people, in order to be able to abjudicate with a title of right regarding the supreme power in the state, must be regarded as already united under one common legislative will, it cannot judge otherwise than as the present supreme head of the state (summus imperans) wills. The question has been raised as to whether an actual contract of subjection (pactum subjectionis civilis) originally preceded the civil government as a fact; or whether the power arose first, and the law only followed afterwards, or may have followed in this order. But such questions, as regards the people already actually living under the civil law, are either entirely aimless, or even fraught with subtle danger to the state. For, should the subject, after having dug down to the ultimate origin of the state, rise in opposition to the present ruling authority, he would expose himself as a citizen, according to the law and with full right, to be punished, destroyed, or outlawed. A law which is so holy and inviolable that it is practically a crime even to cast doubt upon it, or to suspend its operation for a moment, is represented of itself as necessarily derived from some supreme, unblameable lawgiver. And this is the meaning of the maxim, "All authority is from God", which proposition does not express the historical foundation of the civil constitution, but an ideal principle of the practical reason. It may be otherwise rendered thus: "It is a duty to obey the law of the existing legislative power, be its origin what it may."

Hence it follows, that the supreme power in the state has only rights, and no (compulsory) duties towards the subject. Further, if the ruler or regent, as the organ of the supreme power, proceeds in violation of the laws, as in imposing taxes, recruiting soldiers, and so on, contrary to the law of equality in the distribution of the political burdens, the subject may oppose complaints and objections (gravamina) to this injustice, but not active resistance.

There cannot even be an Article contained in the political constitution that would make it possible for a power in the state, in case of the transgression of the constitutional laws by the supreme authority, to resist or even to restrict it in so doing. For, whoever would restrict the supreme power of the state must have more, or at least equal, power as compared with the power that is so restricted; and if competent to command the subjects to resist, such a one would also have to be able to protect them, and if he is to be considered capable of judging what is right in every case, he may also publicly order resistance. But such a one, and not the actual authority, would then be the supreme power; which is contradictory. The supreme sovereign power, then, in proceeding by a minister who is at the same time the ruler of the state, consequently becomes despotic; and the expedient of giving the people to imagine- when they have properly only legislative influence- that they act by their deputies by way of limiting the sovereign authority, cannot so mask and disguise the actual despotism of such a government that it will not appear in the measures and means adopted by the minister to carry out his function. The people, while represented by their deputies in parliament, under such conditions, may have in these warrantors of their freedom and rights, persons who are keenly interested on their own account and their families, and who look to such a minister for the benefit of his influence in the army, navy, and public offices. And hence, instead of offering resistance to the undue pretensions of the government- whose public declarations ought to carry a prior accord on the part of the people, which, however, cannot be allowed in peace, they are rather always ready to play into the hands of the government. Hence the so-called limited political constitution, as a constitution of the internal rights of the state, is an unreality; and instead of being consistent with right, it is only a principle of expediency. And its aim is not so much to throw all possible obstacles in the way of a powerful violator of popular rights by his arbitrary influence upon the government, as rather to cloak it over under the illusion of a right of opposition conceded to the people.

Resistance on the part of the people to the supreme legislative power of the state is in no case legitimate; for it is only by submission to the universal legislative will, that a condition of law and order is possible. Hence there is no right of sedition, and still less of rebellion, belonging to the people. And least of all, when the supreme power is embodied in an individual monarch, is there any justification, under the pretext of his abuse of power, for seizing his person or taking away his life (monarchomachismus sub specie tyrannicidii). The slightest attempt of this kind is high treason (proditio eminens); and a traitor of this sort who aims at the overthrow of his country may be punished, as a political parricide, even with death. It is the duty of the people to bear any abuse of the supreme power, even then though it should be considered to be unbearable. And the reason is that any resistance of the highest legislative authority can never but be contrary to the law, and must even be regarded as tending to destroy the whole legal constitution. In order to be entitled to offer such resistance, a public law would be required to permit it. But the supreme legislation would by such a law cease to be supreme, and the people as subjects would be made sovereign over that to which they are subject; which is a contradiction. And the contradiction becomes more apparent when the question is put: "Who is to be the judge in a controversy between the people and the sovereign?" For the people and the sovereign are to be constitutionally or juridically regarded as two different moral persons; but the question shows that the people would then have to be the judge in their own cause.

The dethronement of a monarch may be also conceived as a voluntary abdication of the crown, and a resignation of his power into the hands of the people; or it might be a deliberate surrender of these without any assault on the royal person, in order that the monarch may be relegated into private life. But, however it happen, forcible compulsion of it, on the part of the people, cannot be justified under the pretext of a right of necessity (casus necessitatis); and least of all can the slightest right be shown for punishing the sovereign on the ground of previous maladministration. For all that has been already done in the quality of a sovereign must be regarded as done outwardly by right; and, considered as the source of the laws, the sovereign himself can do no wrong. Of all the abominations in the overthrow of a state by revolution, even the murder or assassination of the monarch is not the worst. For that may be done by the people out of fear, lest, if he is allowed to live, he may again acquire power and inflict punishment upon them; and so it may be done, not as an act of punitive justice, but merely from regard to self-preservation. It is the formal execution of a monarch that horrifies a soul filled with ideas of human right; and this feeling occurs again and again as of as the mind realizes the scenes that terminated the fate of Charles I or Louis XVI. Now how is this feeling to be explained? It is not a mere aesthetic feeling, arising from the working of the imagination, nor from sympathy, produced by fancying ourselves in the place of the sufferer. On the contrary, it is a moral feeling arising from the entire subversion of all our notions of right. Regicide, in short, is regarded as a crime which always remains such and can never be expiated (crimen immortale, inexpiabile); and it appears to resemble that sin which the theologians declare can neither be forgiven in this world nor in the next. The explanation of this phenomenon in the human mind appears to be furnished by the following reflections upon it; and they even shed some light upon the principles of political right.

Every transgression of a law only can and must be explained as arising from a maxim of the transgressor making such wrong-doing his rule of action; for were it not committed by him as a free being, it could not be imputed to him. But it is absolutely impossible to explain how any rational individual forms such a maxim against the clear prohibition of the law-giving reason; for it is only events which happen according to the mechanical laws of nature that are capable of explanation. Now a transgressor or criminal may commit his wrong-doing either according to the maxim of a rule supposed to be valid objectively and universally, or only as an exception from the rule by dispensing with its obligation for the occasion. In the latter case, he only diverges from the law, although intentionally. He may, at the same time, abhor his own transgression, and without formally renouncing his obedience to the law only wish to avoid it. In the former case, however, he rejects the authority of the law itself, the validity of which, however, he cannot repudiate before his own reason, even while he makes it his rule to act against it. His maxim is, therefore, not merely defective as being negatively contrary to the law, but it is even positively illegal, as being diametrically contrary and in hostile opposition to it.

So far as we can see into and understand the relation, it would appear as if it were impossible for men to commit wrongs and crimes of a wholly useless form of wickedness, and yet the idea of such extreme perversity cannot be overlooked in a system of moral philosophy.

There is thus a feeling of horror at the thought of the formal execution of a monarch by his people. And the reason it is that, whereas an act of assassination must be considered as only an exception from the rule which has been constituted a maxim, such an execution must be regarded as a complete perversion of the principles that should regulate the relation between a sovereign and his people. For it makes the people, who owe their constitutional existence to the legislation that issued from the sovereign, to be the ruler over him. Hence mere violence is thus elevated with bold brow, and as it were by principle, above the holiest right; and, appearing like an abyss to swallow up everything without recall, it seems like suicide committed by the state upon itself and a crime that is capable of no atonement. There is therefore reason to assume that the consent that is accorded to such executions is not really based upon a supposed principle of right, but only springs from fear of the vengeance that would be taken upon the people were the same power to revive again in the state. And hence it may be held that the formalities accompanying them have only been put forward in order to give these deeds a look of punishment from the accompaniment of a judicial process, such as could not go along with a mere murder or assassination. But such a cloaking of the deed entirely fails of its purpose, because this pretension on the part of the people is even worse than murder itself, as it implies a principle which would necessarily make the restoration of a state, when once overthrown, an impossibility.

An alteration of the still defective constitution of the state may sometimes be quite necessary. But all such changes ought only to proceed from the sovereign power in the way of reform, and are not to be brought about by the people in the way of revolution; and when they take place, they should only effect the executive, and not the legislative, power. A political constitution which is so modified that the people by their representatives in parliament can legally resist the executive power, and its representative minister, is called a limited constitution. Yet even under such a constitution there is no right of active resistance, as by an arbitrary combination of the people to coerce the government into a certain active procedure; for this would be to assume to perform an act of the executive itself. All that can rightly be allowed, is only a negative resistance, amounting to an act of refusal on the part of the people to concede all the demands which the executive may deem it necessary to make in behoof of the political administration. And if this right were never exercised, it would be a sure sign that the people were corrupted, their representatives venal, the supreme head of the government despotic, and his ministers practically betrayers of the people.

Further, when on the success of a revolution a new constitution has been founded, the unlawfulness of its beginning and of its institution cannot release the subjects from the obligation of adapting themselves, as good citizens, to the new order of things; and they are not entitled to refuse honourably to obey the authority that has thus attained the power in the state. A dethroned monarch, who has survived such a revolution, is not to be called to account on the ground of his former administration; and still less may he be punished for it, when with drawing into the private life of a citizen he prefers his own quiet and the peace of the state to the uncertainty of exile, with the intention of maintaining his claims for restoration at all hazards, and pushing these either by secret counter-revolution or by the assistance of other powers. However, if he prefers to follow the latter course, his rights remain, because the rebellion that drove him from his position was inherently unjust. But the question then emerges as to whether other powers have the right to form themselves into an alliance in behalf of such a dethroned monarch merely in order not to leave the crime committed by the people unavenged, or to do away with it as a scandal to all the states; and whether they are therefore justified and called upon to restore by force to another state a formerly existing constitution that has been removed by a revolution. The discussion of this question, however, does not belong to this department of public right, but to the following section, concerning the right of nations.

B. Land Rights. Secular and Church Lands, Rights of Taxation;

Finance; Police; Inspection.

Is the sovereign, viewed as embodying the legislative power, to be regarded as the supreme proprietor of the soil, or only as the highest ruler of the people by the laws? As the soil is the supreme condition under which it is alone possible to have external things as one's own, its possible possession and use constitute the first acquirable basis of external right. Hence it is that all such rights must be derived from the sovereign as overlord and paramount superior of the soil, or, as it may be better put, as the supreme proprietor of the land (dominus territorii). The people, as forming the mass of the subjects, belong to the sovereign as a people; not in the sense of his being their proprietor in the way of real right, but as their supreme commander or chief in the way of personal right. This supreme proprietorship, however, is only an idea of the civil constitution, objectified to represent, in accordance with juridical conceptions, the necessary union of the private property of all the people under a public universal possessor. The relation is so represented in order that it may form a basis for the determination of particular rights in property. It does not proceed, therefore, upon the principle of mere aggregation, which advances empirically from the parts to the whole, but from the necessary formal principle of a division of the soil according to conceptions of right. In accordance with this principle, the supreme universal proprietor cannot have any private property in any part of the soil; for otherwise he would make himself a private person. Private property in the soil belongs only to the people, taken distributively and not collectively; from which condition, however, a nomadic people must be excepted as having no private property at all in the soil. The supreme proprietor accordingly ought not to hold private estates, either for private use or for the support of the court. For, as it would depend upon his own pleasure how far these should extend, the state would be in danger of seeing all property in the land taken into the hands of the government, and all the subjects treated as bondsmen of the soil (glebae adscripti). As possessors only of what was the private property of another, they might thus be deprived of all freedom and regarded as serfs or slaves. Of the supreme proprietor of the land, it may be said that he possesses nothing as his own, except himself; for if he possessed things in the state alongside of others, dispute and litigation would be possible with these others regarding those things, and there would be no independent judge to settle the cause. But it may also be said that he possesses everything; for he has the supreme right of sovereignty over the whole people, to whom all external things severally (divisim) belong; and as such he assigns distributively to every one what is to be his.

Hence there cannot be any corporation in the state, nor any class or order, that as proprietors can transmit the land for a sole exclusive use to the following generations for all time (ad infinitum), according to certain fixed statutes. The state may annul and abrogate all such statutes at any time, only under the condition of indemnifying survivors for their interests. The order of knights, constituting the nobility regarded as a mere rank or class of specially titled individuals, as well as the order of the clergy, called the church, are both subject to this relation. They can never be entitled by any hereditary privileges with which they may be favoured, to acquire an absolute property in the soil transmissible to their successors. They can only acquire the use of such property for the time being. If public opinion has ceased, on account of other arrangements, to impel the state to protect itself from negligence in the national defence by appeal to the military honour of the knightly order, the estates granted on that condition may be recalled. And, in like manner, the church lands or spiritualities may be reclaimed by the state without scruple, if public opinion has ceased to impel the members of the state to maintain masses for the souls of the dead, prayers for the living, and a multitude of clergy, as means to protect themselves from eternal fire. But in both cases, the condition of indemnifying existing interests must be observed. Those who in this connection fall under the movement of reform are not entitled to complain that their property is taken from them; for the foundation of their previous possession lay only in the opinion of the people, and it can be valid only so long as this opinion lasts. As soon as this public opinion in favour of such institutions dies out, or is even extinguished in the judgement of those who have the greatest claim by their acknowledged merit to lead and represent it, the putative proprietorship in question must cease, as if by a public appeal made regarding it to the state (a rege male informato ad regem melius informandum).

On this primarily acquired supreme proprietorship in the land rests the right of the sovereign, as universal proprietor of the country, to assess the private proprietors of the soil, and to demand taxes, excise, and dues, or the performance of service to the state such as may be required in war. But this is to be done so that it is actually the people that assess themselves, this being the only mode of proceeding according to laws of right. This may be effected through the medium of the body of deputies who represent the people. It is also permissible, in circumstances in which the state is in imminent danger, to proceed by a forced loan, as a right vested in the sovereign, although this may be a divergence from the existing law.

Upon this principle is also founded the right of administering the national economy, including the finance and the police. The police has specially to care for the public safety, convenience, and decency. As regards the last of these- the feeling or negative taste for public propriety- it is important that it be not deadened by such influences as begging, disorderly noises, offensive smells, public prostitution (Venus vulgivaga), or other offences against the moral sense, as it greatly facilitates the government in the task of regulating the life of the people by law.

For the preservation of the state there further belongs to it a right of inspection (jus inspectionis), which entitles the public authority to see that no secret society, political or religious, exists among the people that can exert a prejudicial influence upon the public weal. Accordingly, when it is required by the police, no such secret society may refuse to lay open its constitution. But the visitation and search of private houses by the police can only be justified in a case of necessity; and in every particular instance, it must be authorized by a higher authority.

C. Relief of the Poor. Foundling Hospitals. The Church.

The sovereign, as undertaker of the duty of the people, has the right to tax them for purposes essentially connected with their own preservation. Such are, in particular, the relief of the poor, foundling asylums, and ecclesiastical establishments, otherwise designated charitable or pious foundations.

1. The people have in fact united themselves by their common will into a society, which has to be perpetually maintained; and for this purpose they have subjected themselves to the internal power of the state, in order to preserve the members of this society even when they are not able to support themselves. By the fundamental principle of the state, the government is justified and entitled to

compel those who are able, to furnish the means necessary to preserve those who are not themselves capable of providing for the most necessary wants of nature. For the existence of persons with property in the state implies their submission under it for protection and the provision by the state of what is necessary for their existence; and accordingly the state founds a right upon an obligation on their part to contribute of their means for the preservation of their fellow citizens. This may be carried out by taxing the property or the commercial industry of the citizens, or by establishing funds and drawing interest from them, not for the wants of the state as such, which is rich, but for those of the people. And this is not to be done merely by voluntary contributions, but by compulsory exactions as state-burdens, for we are here considering only the right of the state in relation to the people. Among the voluntary modes of raising such contributions, lotteries ought not to be allowed, because they increase the number of those who are poor, and involve danger to the public property. It may be asked whether the relief of the poor ought to be administered out of current contributions, so that every age should maintain its own poor; or whether this were better done by means of permanent funds and charitable institutions, such as widows' homes, hospitals, etc.? And if the former method is the better, it may also be considered whether the means necessary are to be raised by a legal assessment rather than by begging, which is generally nigh akin to robbing. The former method must in reality be regarded as the only one that is conformable to the right of the state, which cannot withdraw its connection from any one who has to live. For a legal current provision does not make the profession of poverty a means of gain for the indolent, as is to be feared is the case with pious foundations when they grow with the number of the poor; nor can it be charged with being an unjust or unrighteous burden imposed by the government on the people.

2. The state has also a right to impose upon the people the duty of preserving children exposed from want or shame, and who would otherwise perish; for it cannot knowingly allow this increase of its power to be destroyed, however unwelcome in some respects it may be. But it is a difficult question to determine how this may most justly be carried out. It might be considered whether it would not be right to exact contributions for this purpose from the unmarried persons of both sexes who are possessed of means, as being in part responsible for the evil; and further, whether the end in view would be best carried out by foundling hospitals, or in what other way consistent with right. But this is a problem of which no solution has yet been offered that does not in some measure offend against right or morality.

3. The church is here regarded as an ecclesiastical establishment merely, and as such it must be carefully distinguished from religion, which as an internal mode of feeling lies wholly beyond the sphere of the action of the civil power. Viewed as an

institution for public worship founded for the people- to whose opinion or conviction it owes its origin- the church establishment responds to a real want in the state. This is the need felt by the people to regard themselves as also subjects of a Supreme Invisible Power to which they must pay homage, and which may of be brought into a very undesirable collision with the civil power. The state has therefore a right in this relation; but it is not to be regarded as the right of constitutional legislation in the church, so as to organize it as may seem most advantageous for itself, or to prescribe and command its faith and ritual forms of worship (ritus); for all this must be left entirely to the teachers and rulers which the church has chosen for itself. The function of the state in this connection, only includes the negative right of regulating the influence of these public teachers upon the visible political commonwealth, that it may not be prejudicial to the public peace and tranquility. Consequently the state has to take measures, on occasion of any internal conflict in the church, or on occasion of any collision of the several churches with each other, that civil concord is not endangered; and this right falls within the province of the police. It is beneath the dignity of the supreme power to interpose in determining what particular faith the church shall profess, or to decree that a certain faith shall be unalterably held, and that the church may not reform itself. For in doing so, the supreme power would be mixing itself up in a scholastic wrangle, on a footing of equality with its subjects; the monarch would be making himself a priest; and the churchmen might even reproach the supreme power with understanding nothing about matters of faith. Especially would this hold in respect of any prohibition of internal reform in the church; for what the people as a whole cannot determine upon for themselves cannot be determined for the people by the legislator. But no people can ever rationally determine that they will never advance farther in their insight into matters of faith, or resolve that they will never reform the institutions of the church; because this would be opposed to the humanity in their own persons and to their highest rights. And therefore the supreme power cannot of itself resolve and decree in these matters for the people. As regards the cost of maintaining the ecclesiastical establishment, for similar reasons this must be derived not from the public funds of the state, but from the section of the people who profess the particular faith of the church; and thus only ought it to fall as a burden on the community.

D. The Right of Assigning Offices and Dignities in the State.

The right of the supreme authority in the state also includes:

1. The distribution of offices, as public and paid employments;

2. The conferring of dignities, as unpaid distinctions of rank, founded merely on honour, but establishing a gradation of higher and lower orders in the political scale; the latter, although free in themselves, being under obligation determined by the

public law to obey the former so far as they are also entitled to command;

3. Besides these relatively beneficent rights, the supreme power in the state is also invested with the right of administering punishment.

As regards civil offices, the question arises as to whether the sovereign has the right, after bestowing an office on an individual, to take it again away at his mere pleasure, without any crime having been committed by the holder of the office. I say, "No." For what the united will of the people would never resolve, regarding their civil officers, cannot (constitutionally) be determined by the sovereign regarding them. The people have to bear the cost incurred by the appointment of an official, and undoubtedly it must be their will that any one in office should be completely competent for its duties. But such competency can only be acquired by a long preparation and training, and this process would necessarily occupy the time that would be required for acquiring the means of support by a different occupation. Arbitrary and frequent changes would therefore, as a rule, have the effect of filling offices with functionaries who have not acquired the skill required for their duties, and whose judgements had not attained maturity by practice. All this is contrary to the purpose of the state. And besides it is requisite in the interest of the people that it should be possible for every individual to rise from a lower office to the higher offices, as these latter would otherwise fall into incompetent hands, and that competent officials generally should have some guarantee of life-long provision.

Civil dignities include not only such as are connected with a public office, but also those which make the possessors of them, without any accompanying services to the state, members of a higher class or rank. The latter constitute the nobility, whose members are distinguished from the common citizens who form the mass of the people. The rank of the nobility is inherited by male descendants; and these again communicate it to wives who are not nobly born. Female descendants of noble families, however, do not communicate their rank to husbands who are not of noble birth, but they descend themselves into the common civil status of the people. This being so, the question then emerges as to whether the sovereign has the right to found a hereditary rank and class, intermediate between himself and the other citizens? The import of this question does not turn on whether it is conformable to the prudence of the sovereign, from regard to his own and the people's interests, to have such an institution; but whether it is in accordance with the right of the people that they should have a class of persons above them, who, while being subjects like themselves, are yet born as their commanders, or at least as privileged superiors? The answer to this question, as in previous instances, is to be derived from the principle that "what the people, as constituting the whole mass of the subjects, could not determine regarding themselves and their associated citizens, cannot be constitutionally determined by the sovereign regarding the people." Now a hereditary nobility is a rank which takes precedence of merit and is hoped for without any good reason- a thing of the imagination without genuine reality. For if an ancestor had merit, he could not transmit it to his posterity, but they must always acquire it for themselves. Nature has in fact not so arranged that the talent and will which give rise to merit in the state, are hereditary. And because it cannot be supposed of any individual that he will throw away his freedom, it is impossible that the common will of all the people should agree to such a groundless prerogative, and hence the sovereign cannot make it valid. It may happen, however, that such an anomaly as that of subjects who would be more than citizens, in the manner of born officials, or hereditary professors, has slipped into the mechanism of government in olden times, as in the case of the feudal system, which was almost entirely organized with reference to war. Under such circumstances, the state cannot deal otherwise with this error of a wrongly instituted rank in its midst, than by the remedy of a gradual extinction through hereditary positions being left unfilled as they fall vacant. The state has therefore the right provisorily to let a dignity in title continue, until the public opinion matures on the subject. And this will thus pass from the threefold division into sovereign, nobles, and people, to the twofold and only natural division into sovereign and people.

No individual in the state can indeed be entirely without dignity; for he has at least that of being a citizen, except when he has lost his civil status by a crime. As a criminal he is still maintained in life, but he is made the mere instrument of the will of another, whether it be the state or a particular citizen. In the latter position, in which he could only be placed by a juridical judgement, he would practically become a slave, and would belong as property (dominium) to another, who would be not merely his master (herus) but his owner (dominus). Such an owner would be entitled to exchange or alienate him as a thing, to use him at will except for shameful purposes, and to dispose of his powers, but not of his life and members. No one can bind himself to such a condition of dependence, as he would thereby cease to be a person, and it is only as a person that he can make a contract. It may, however, appear that one man may bind himself to another by a contract of hire, to discharge a certain service that is permissible in its kind, but is left entirely undetermined as regards its measure or amount; and that as receiving wages or board or protection in return, he thus becomes only a servant subject to the will of a master (subditus) and not a slave (servus). But this is an illusion. For if masters are entitled to use the powers of such subjects at will, they may exhaust these powers- as has been done in the case of Negroes in the Sugar Island- and they may thus reduce their servants to despair and death. But this would imply that they had actually given themselves away to their masters as property; which, in the case of persons, is impossible. A person can, therefore, only contract to perform work that is defined both in quality and quantity, either as a day-labourer or as a domiciled subject. In the latter case he may enter into a contract of lease for the use of the land of a superior, giving a definite rent or annual return for its utilization by himself, or he may contract for his service as a labourer upon the land. But he does not thereby make himself a slave, or a bondsman, or a serf attached to the soil (glebae adscriptus), as he would thus divest himself of his personality; he can only enter into a temporary or at most a heritable lease. And even if by committing a crime he has personally become subjected to another, this subject-condition does not become hereditary; for he has only brought it upon himself by his own wrongdoing. Neither can one who has been begotten by a slave be claimed as property on the ground of the cost of his rearing, because such rearing is an absolute duty naturally incumbent upon parents; and in case the parents be slaves, it devolves upon their masters or owners, who, in undertaking the possession of such subjects, have also made themselves responsible for the performance of their duties.

E. The Right of Punishing and of Pardoning.

I. The Right of Punishing.

The right of administering punishment is the right of the sovereign as the supreme power to inflict pain upon a subject on account of a crime committed by him. The head of the state cannot therefore be punished; but his supremacy may be withdrawn from him. Any transgression of the public law which makes him who commits it incapable of being a citizen, constitutes a crime, either simply as a private crime (crimen), or also as a public crime (crimen publicum). Private crimes are dealt with by a civil court; public crimes by a criminal court. Embezzlement or speculation of money or goods entrusted in trade, fraud in purchase or sale, if done before the eyes of the party who suffers, are private crimes. On the other hand, coining false money or forging bills of exchange, theft, robbery, etc., are public crimes, because the commonwealth, and not merely some particular individual, is endangered thereby. Such crimes may be divided into those of a base character (indolis abjectae) and those of a violent character (indolis violentiae).

Judicial or juridical punishment (poena forensis) is to be distinguished from natural punishment (poena naturalis), in which crime as vice punishes itself, and does not as such come within the cognizance of the legislator. juridical punishment can never be administered merely as a means for promoting another good either with regard to the criminal himself or to civil society, but must in all cases be imposed only because the individual on whom it is inflicted has committed a crime. For one man ought never to be dealt with merely as a means subservient to the purpose of another, nor be mixed up with the subjects of real right. Against such treatment his inborn personality has a right to protect him, even although he may be condemned to lose his civil personality. He must first be found guilty and punishable, before there can be any thought of drawing from his punishment any benefit for himself or his fellow-citizens. The penal law is a categorical imperative; and woe to him who creeps through the serpent-windings of utilitarianism to discover some advantage that may discharge him from the justice of punishment, or even from the due measure of it, according to the Pharisaic maxim: "It is better that one man should die than that the whole people should perish." For if justice and righteousness perish, human life would no longer have any value in the world. What, then, is to be said of such a proposal as to keep a criminal alive who has been condemned to death, on his being given to understand that, if he agreed to certain dangerous experiments being performed upon him, he would be allowed to survive if he came happily through them? It is argued that physicians might thus obtain new information that would be of value to the commonweal. But a court of justice would repudiate with scorn any proposal of this kind if made to it by the medical faculty; for justice would cease to be justice, if it were bartered away for any consideration whatever.

But what is the mode and measure of punishment which public justice takes as its principle and standard? It is just the principle of equality, by which the pointer of the scale of justice is made to incline no more to the one side than the other. It may be rendered by saying that the undeserved evil which any one commits on another is to be regarded as perpetrated on himself. Hence it may be said: "If you slander another, you slander yourself; if you steal from another, you steal from yourself; if you strike another, you strike yourself; if you kill another, you kill yourself." This is the right of retaliation (jus talionis); and, properly understood, it is the only principle which in regulating a public court, as distinguished from mere private judgement, can definitely assign both the quality and the quantity of a just penalty. All other standards are wavering and uncertain; and on account of other considerations involved in them, they contain no principle conformable to the sentence of pure and strict justice. It may appear, however, that difference of social status would not admit the application of the principle of retaliation, which is that of "like with like." But although the application may not in all cases be possible according to the letter, yet as regards the effect it may always be attained in practice, by due regard being given to the disposition and sentiment of the parties in the higher social sphere. Thus a pecuniary penalty on account of a verbal injury may have no direct proportion to the injustice of slander; for one who is wealthy may be able to indulge himself in this offence for his own gratification. Yet the attack committed on the honour of the party aggrieved may have its equivalent in the pain inflicted upon the pride of the aggressor, especially if he is condemned by the judgement of the court, not only to retract and apologize, but to submit to some meaner ordeal, as kissing the hand of the injured person. In like manner, if a man of the highest rank has violently assaulted an innocent citizen of the lower orders, he may be condemned not only to apologize but to undergo a solitary and painful imprisonment, whereby, in addition to the discomfort endured, the vanity of the offender would be painfully affected, and the very shame of his position would constitute an adequate retaliation after the principle of "like with like." But how then would we render the statement: "If you steal from another, you steal from yourself?" In this way, that whoever steals anything makes the property of all insecure; he therefore robs himself of all security in property, according to the right of retaliation. Such a one has nothing, and can acquire nothing, but he has the will to live; and this is only possible by others supporting him. But as the state should not do this gratuitously, he must for this purpose yield his powers to the state to be used in penal labour; and thus he falls for a time, or it may be for life, into a condition of slavery. But whoever has committed murder, must die. There is, in this case, no juridical substitute or surrogate, that can be given or taken for the satisfaction of justice. There is no likeness or proportion between life, however painful, and death; and therefore there is no equality between the crime of murder and the retaliation of it but what is judicially accomplished by the execution of the criminal. His death, however, must be kept free from all maltreatment that would make the humanity suffering in his person loathsome or abominable. Even if a civil society resolved to dissolve itself with the consent of all its members- as might be supposed in the case of a people inhabiting an island resolving to separate and scatter themselves throughout the whole world- the last murderer lying in the prison ought to be executed before the resolution was carried out. This ought to be done in order that every one may realize the desert of his deeds, and that blood-guiltiness may not remain upon the people; for otherwise they might all be regarded as participators in the murder as a public violation of justice.

The equalization of punishment with crime is therefore only possible by the cognition of the judge extending even to the penalty of death, according to the right of retaliation. This is manifest from the fact that it is only thus that a sentence can be pronounced over all criminals proportionate to their internal wickedness; as may be seen by considering the case when the punishment of death has to be inflicted, not on account of a murder, but on account of a political crime that can only be punished capitally. A hypothetical case, founded on history, will illustrate this. In the last Scottish rebellion there were various participators in it- such as Balmerino and others- who believed that in taking part in the rebellion they were only discharging their duty to the house of Stuart; but there were also others who were animated only by private motives and interests. Now, suppose that the judgement of the supreme court regarding them had been this: that every one should have liberty to choose between the punishment of death or penal servitude for life. In view of such an alternative, I say that the man of honour would choose death, and the knave would choose servitude. This would be the effect of their human nature as it is; for the honourable man values his honour more highly than even life itself, whereas a knave regards a life, although covered with shame, as better in his eyes than not to be. The former is, without gainsaying, less guilty than the other; and they can only be proportionately punished by death being inflicted equally upon them both; yet to the one it is a mild punishment when his nobler temperament is taken into account, whereas it is a hard punishment to the other in view of his baser temperament. But, on the other hand, were they all equally condemned to penal servitude for life, the honourable man would be too severely punished, while the other, on account of his baseness of nature, would be too mildly punished. In the judgement to be pronounced over a number of criminals united in such a conspiracy, the best equalizer of punishment and crime in the form of public justice is death. And besides all this, it has never been heard of that a criminal condemned to death on account of a murder has complained that the sentence inflicted on him more than was right and just; and any one would treat him with scorn if he expressed himself to this effect against it. Otherwise it would be necessary to admit that, although wrong and injustice are not done to the criminal by the law, yet the legislative power is not entitled to administer this mode of punishment; and if it did so, it would be in contradiction with itself.

However many they may be who have committed a murder, or have even commanded it, or acted as art and part in it, they ought all to suffer death; for so justice wills it, in accordance with the idea of the juridical power, as founded on the universal laws of reason. But the number of the accomplices (correi) in such a deed might happen to be so great that the state, in resolving to be without such criminals, would be in danger of soon also being deprived of subjects. But it will not thus dissolve itself, neither must it return to the much worse condition of nature, in which there would be no external justice. Nor, above all, should it deaden the sensibilities of the people by the spectacle of justice being exhibited in the mere carnage of a slaughtering bench. In such circumstances the sovereign must always be allowed to have it in his power to take the part of the judge upon himself as a case of necessity- and to deliver a judgement which, instead of the penalty of death, shall assign some other punishment to the criminals and thereby preserve a multitude of the people. The penalty of deportation is relevant in this connection. Such a form of judgement cannot be carried out according to a public law, but only by an authoritative act of the royal prerogative, and it may only be applied as an act of grace in individual cases.

Against these doctrines, the Marquis Beccaria has given forth a different view. Moved by the compassionate sentimentality of a humane feeling, he has asserted that all capital punishment is wrong in itself and unjust. He has put forward this view on the ground that the penalty of death could not be contained in the original civil contract; for, in that case, every one of the people would have had to consent to lose his life if be murdered any of his fellow citizens. But, it is argued, such a consent is impossible, because no one can thus dispose of his own life. All this is mere sophistry and perversion of right. No one undergoes punishment because he has willed to be punished, but because he has willed a punishable action; for it is in fact no punishment when any one experiences what he wills, and it is impossible for any one to will to be punished. To say, "I will to be punished, if I murder any one," can mean nothing more than, "I submit myself along with all the other citizens to the laws"; and if there are any criminals among the people, these laws will include penal laws. The individual who, as a co-legislator, enacts penal law cannot possibly be the same person who, as a subject, is punished according to the law; for, qua criminal, he cannot possibly be regarded as having a voice in the legislation, the legislator being rationally viewed as just and holy. If any one, then, enact a penal law against himself as a criminal, it must be the pure juridically law-giving reason (homo noumenon), which subjects him as one capable of crime, and consequently as another person (homo phenomenon), along with all the others in the civil union, to this penal law. In other words, it is not the people taken distributively, but the tribunal of public justice, as distinct from the criminal, that prescribes capital punishment; and it is not to be viewed as if the social contract contained the promise of all the individuals to allow themselves to be punished, thus disposing of themselves and their lives. For if the right to punish must be grounded upon a promise of the wrongdoer, whereby he is to be regarded as being willing to be punished, it ought also to be left to him to find himself deserving of the punishment; and the criminal would thus be his own judge. The chief error (proton pseudos) of this sophistry consists in regarding the judgement of the criminal himself, necessarily determined by his reason, that he is under obligation to undergo the loss of his life, as a judgement that must be grounded on a resolution of his will to take it away himself; and thus the execution of the right in question is represented as united in one and the same person with the adjudication of the right.

There are, however, two crimes worthy of death, in respect of which it still remains doubtful whether the legislature have the right to deal with them capitally. It is the sentiment of honour that induces their perpetration. The one originates in a regard for womanly honour, the other in a regard for military honour; and in both cases there is a genuine feeling of honour incumbent on the individuals as a duty. The former is the crime of maternal infanticide (infanticidium maternale); the latter is the crime of killing a fellow-soldier in a duel (commilitonicidium). Now legislation cannot take away the shame of an illegitimate birth, nor wipe off the stain attaching from a suspicion of cowardice, to an officer who does not resist an act that would bring him into contempt, by an effort of his own that is superior to the fear of death. Hence it appears that, in such circumstances, the individuals concerned are remitted to the state of nature; and their acts in both cases must be called homicide, and not murder, which involves evil intent (homicidium dolosum). In all instances the acts are undoubtedly punishable; but they cannot be punished by the supreme power with death. An illegitimate child comes into the world outside of the law which properly regulates marriage, and it is thus born beyond the pale or constitutional protection of the law. Such a child is introduced, as it were, like prohibited goods, into the commonwealth, and as it has no legal right to existence in this way, its destruction might also be ignored; nor can the shame of the mother, when her unmarried confinement is known, be removed by any legal ordinance. A subordinate officer, again, on whom an insult is inflicted, sees himself compelled by the public opinion of his associates to obtain satisfaction; and, as in the state of nature, the punishment of the offender can only be effected by a duel, in which his own life is exposed to danger, and not by means of the law in a court of justice. The duel is therefore adopted as the means of demonstrating his courage as that characteristic upon which the honour of his profession essentially rests; and this is done even if it should issue in the killing of his adversary. But as such a result takes place publicly and under the consent of both parties, although it may be done unwillingly, it cannot properly be called murder (homicidium dolosum). What then is the right in both cases as relating to criminal justice? Penal justice is here in fact brought into great straits, having apparently either to declare the notion of honour, which is certainly no mere fancy here, to 'be nothing in the eye of the law, or to exempt the crime from its due punishment; and thus it would become either remiss or cruel. The knot thus tied is to be resolved in the following way. The categorical imperative of penal justice, that the killing of any person contrary to the law must be punished with death, remains in force; but the legislation itself and the civil constitution generally, so long as they are still barbarous and incomplete, are at fault. And this is the reason why the subjective motive-principles of honour among the people do not coincide with the standards which are objectively conformable to another purpose; so that the public justice issuing from the state becomes injustice relatively to that which is upheld among the people themselves.

II. The Right of Pardoning.

The right of pardoning (jus aggratiandi), viewed in relation to the criminal, is the right of mitigating or entirely remitting his punishment. On the side of the sovereign this is the most delicate of all rights, as it may be exercised so as to set forth the splendour of his dignity, and yet so as to do a great wrong by it. It ought not to be exercised in application to the crimes of the subjects against each other;

for exemption from punishment (impunitas criminis) would be the greatest wrong that could be done to them. It is only an occasion of some form of treason (crimen laesae majestatis), as a lesion against himself, that the sovereign should make use of this right. And it should not be exercised even in this connection, if the safety of the people would be endangered by remitting such punishment. This right is the only one which properly deserves the name of a "right of majesty."

50. Juridical Relations of the Citizen to his Country and
to Other Countries. Emigration; Immigration; Banishment;
Exile.

The land or territory whose inhabitants- in virtue of its political constitution and without the necessary intervention of a special juridical act- are, by birth, fellow-citizens of one and the same commonwealth, is called their country or fatherland. A foreign country is one in which they would not possess this condition, but would be living abroad. If a country abroad form part of the territory under the same government as at home, it constitutes a province, according to the Roman usage of the term. It does not constitute an incorporated portion of the empire (imperii) so as to be the abode of equal fellow-citizens, but is only a possession of the government, like a lower house; and it must therefore honour the domain of the ruling state as the "mother country" (regio domina).

1. A subject, even regarded as a citizen, has the right of emigration; for the state cannot retain him as if he were its property. But he may only carry away with him his moveables as distinguished from his fixed possessions. However, he is entitled to sell his immovable property, and take the value of it in money with him.

2. The supreme power, as master of the country, has the right to favour immigration and the settlement of strangers and colonists. This will hold even although the natives of the country may be unfavourably disposed to it, if their private property in the soil is not diminished or interfered with.

3. In the case of a subject who has committed a crime that renders all society of his fellow-citizens with him prejudicial to the state, the supreme power has also the right of inflicting banishment to a country abroad. By such deportation, he does not acquire any share in the rights of citizens of the territory to which he is banished.

4. The supreme power has also the right of imposing exile generally (jus exilii), by which a citizen is sent abroad into the wide world as the "out-land." And because the supreme authority thus withdraws all legal protection from the citizen, this amounts to making him an "outlaw" within the territory of his own country.

51. The Three Forms of the State: Autocracy;
Aristocracy; Democracy.

The three powers in the state, involved in the conception of a public government generally (res publica latius dicta), are only so many relations of the united will of the people which emanates from the a priori reason; and viewed as such it is the objective practical realization of the pure idea of a supreme head of the state. This supreme head is the sovereign; but conceived only as a representation of the whole people, the idea still requires physical embodiment in a person, who may exhibit the supreme power of the state and bring the idea actively to bear upon the popular will. The relation of the supreme power to the people is conceivable in three different forms: either one in the state rules over all; or some, united in relation of equality with each other, rule over all the others; or all together rule over each and all individually, including themselves. The form of the state is therefore either autocratic, or aristocratic, or democratic. The expression monarchic is not so suitable as autocratic for the conception here intended; for a monarch is one who has the highest power, an autocrat is one who has all power, so that this latter is the sovereign, whereas the former merely represents the sovereignty.

It is evident that an autocracy is the simplest form of government in the state, being constituted by the relation of one, as king, to the people, so that there is one only who is the lawgiver. An aristocracy, as a form of government, is, however, compounded of the union of two relations: that of the nobles in relation to one another as the lawgivers, thereby constituting the sovereignty, and that of this sovereign power to the people. A democracy, again, is the most complex of all the forms of the state, for it has to begin by uniting the will of all so as to form a people; and then it has to appoint a sovereign over this common union, which sovereign is no other than the united will itself. The consideration of the ways in which these forms are adulterated by the intrusion of violent and illegitimate usurpers of power, as in oligarchy and ochlocracy, as well as the discussion of the so called mixed constitutions, may be passed over here as not essential, and as leading into too much detail.

As regards the administration of right in the state, it may be said that the simplest mode is also the best; but as regards its bearing on right itself, it is also the most dangerous for the people, in view of the despotism to which simplicity of administration so naturally gives rise. It is undoubtedly a rational maxim to aim at simplification in the machinery which is to unite the people under compulsory laws, and this would be secured were all the people to be passive and to obey only one person over them; but the method would not give subjects who were also citizens of the state. It is sometimes said that the people should be satisfied with the reflection that monarchy, regarded as an autocracy, is the best political constitution, if the monarch is good, that is, if be has the judgement as well as the will to do right. But this is a mere evasion and belongs to the common class of wise tautological phrases. It only amounts to saying that "the best constitution is that by which the supreme administrator of the state is made the best ruler"; that is, that the best constitution is the best!

52. Historical Origin and Changes.

A Pure Republic. Representative Government.

It is vain to inquire into the historical origin of the political mechanism; for it is no longer possible to discover historically the point of time at which civil society took its beginning. Savages do not draw up a documentary record of their having submitted themselves to law; and it may be inferred from the nature of uncivilized men that they must have set out from a state of violence. To prosecute such an inquiry in the intention of finding a pretext for altering the existing constitution by violence is no less than penal. For such a mode of alteration would amount to revolution, that could only be carried out by an insurrection of the people, and not by constitutional modes of legislation. But insurrection against an already existing constitution, is an overthrow of all civil and juridical relations, and of right generally; and hence it is not a mere alteration of the civil constitution, but a dissolution of it. It would thus form a mode of transition to a better constitution by palingenesis and not by mere metamorphosis; and it would require a new social contract, upon which the former original contract, as then annulled, would have no influence.

It must, however, be possible for the sovereign to change the existing constitution, if it is not actually consistent with the idea of the original contract. In doing so it is essential to give existence to that form of government which will properly constitute the people into a state. Such a change cannot be made by the state deliberately altering its constitution from one of the three forms to one of the other two. For example, political changes should not be carried out by the aristocrats combining to subject themselves to an autocracy, or resolving to fuse all into a democracy, or conversely; as if it depended on the arbitrary choice and liking of the sovereign what constitution he may impose on the people. For, even if as sovereign he resolved to alter the constitution into a democracy, he might be doing wrong to the people, because they might hold such a constitution in abhorrence, and regard either of the other two as more suitable to them in the circumstances.

The forms of the state are only the letter (littera) of the original constitution in the civil union; and they may therefore remain so long as they are considered, from ancient and long habit (and therefore only subjectively), to be necessary to the machinery of the political constitution. But the spirit of that original contract (anima pacti originarii) contains and imposes the obligation on the constituting power to make the mode of the government conformable to its idea; and, if this cannot be effected at once, to change it gradually and continuously till it harmonize in its working with the only rightful constitution, which is that of a pure republic. Thus the old empirical and statutory forms, which serve only to effect the political subjection of the people, will be resolved into the original and rational forms which alone take freedom as their principle, and even as the condition of all compulsion and constraint. Compulsion is in fact requisite for the realization of a juridical constitution, according to the proper idea of the state; and it will lead at last to the realization of that idea, even according to the letter. This is the only enduring political constitution, as in it the law is itself sovereign, and is no longer attached to a particular person. This is the ultimate end of all public right, and the state in which every citizen can have what is his own peremptorily assigned to him. But so long as the form of the state has to be represented, according to the letter, by many different moral persons invested with the supreme power, there can only be a provisory internal right, and not an absolutely juridical state of civil society.

Every true republic is and can only be constituted by a representative system of the people. Such a representative system is instituted in name of the people, and is constituted by all the citizens being united together, in order, by means of their deputies, to protect and secure their rights. But as soon as a supreme head of the state in person- be it as king, or nobility, or the whole body of the people in a democratic union- becomes also representative, the united people then does not merely represent the sovereignty; but they are themselves sovereign. It is in the people that the supreme power originally resides, and it is accordingly from this power that all the rights of individual citizens as mere subjects, and especially as officials of the state, must be derived. When the sovereignty of the people themselves is thus realized, the republic is established; and it is no longer necessary to give up the reins of government into the hands of those by whom they have been hitherto held, especially as they might again destroy all the new institutions by their arbitrary and absolute will.

It was therefore a great error in judgement on the part of a powerful ruler in our time, when he tried to extricate himself from the embarrassment arising from great public debts, by transferring this burden to the people, and leaving them to undertake and distribute them among themselves as they might best think fit. It thus became natural that the legislative power, not only in respect of the taxation of the subjects, but in respect of the government, should come into the hands of the people. It was requisite that they should be able to prevent the incurring of new debts by extravagance or war; and in consequence, the supreme power of the monarch entirely disappeared, not by being merely suspended, but by passing over in fact to the people, to whose legislative will the property of every subject thus became subjected. Nor can it be said that a tacit and yet obligatory promise must be assumed as having, under such circumstances, been given by the national assembly, not to constitute themselves into a sovereignty, but only to administer the affairs of the sovereign for the time, and after this was done to deliver the reins of the government again into the monarch's hands. Such a supposed contract would be null and void. The right of the supreme legislation in the commonwealth is not an alienable right, but is the most personal of all rights. Whoever possesses it can only dispose by the collective will of the people, in respect of the people; he cannot dispose in respect of the collective will itself, which is the ultimate foundation of all public contracts. A contract, by which the people would be bound to give back their authority again, would not be consistent with their position as a legislative power, and yet it would be made binding upon the people; which, on the principle that "No one can serve two masters," is a contradiction.

II. The Right of Nations and International Law.

(Jus Gentium).

53. Nature and Division of the Right of Nations.

The individuals, who make up a people, may be regarded as natives of the country sprung by natural descent from a common ancestry (congeniti), although this may not hold entirely true in detail. Again, they may be viewed according to the intellectual and juridical relation, as born of a common political mother, the republic, so that they constitute, as it were, a public family or nation (gens, natio) whose members are all related to each other as citizens of the state. As members of a state, they do not mix with those who live beside them in the state of nature, considering such to be ignoble. Yet these savages, on account of the lawless freedom they have chosen, regard themselves as superior to civilized peoples; and they constitute tribes and even races, but not states. The public right of states (jus publicum civitatum), in their relations to one another, is what we have to consider under the designation of the "right of nations." Wherever a state, viewed as a moral person, acts in relation to another existing in the condition of natural freedom, and consequently in a state of continual war, such right takes it rise.

The right of nations in relation to the state of war may be divided into: 1. the right of going to war; 2. right during war; and 3. right after war, the object of which is to constrain the nations mutually to pass from this state of war and to found a common constitution establishing perpetual peace. The difference between the right of individual men or families as related to each other in the state of nature, and the right of the nations among themselves, consists in this, that in the right of nations we have to consider not merely a relation of one state to another as a whole, but also the relation of the individual persons in one state to the individuals of another state, as well as to that state as a whole. This difference, however, between the right of nations and the right of individuals in the mere state of nature, requires to be determined by elements which can easily be deduced from the conception of the latter.

54. Elements of the Right of Nations.

The elements of the right of nations are as follows:

1. States, viewed as nations, in their external relations to one another- like lawless savages- are naturally in a non-juridical condition;

2. This natural condition is a state of war in which the right of the stronger prevails; and although it may not in fact be always found as a state of actual war and incessant hostility, and although no real wrong is done to any one therein, yet the condition is wrong in itself in the highest degree, and the nations which form states contiguous to each other are bound mutually to pass out of it;

3. An alliance of nations, in accordance with the idea of an original social contract, is necessary to protect each other against external aggression and attack, but not involving interference with their several internal difficulties and disputes;

4. This mutual connection by alliance must dispense with a distinct sovereign power, such as is set up in the civil constitution; it can only take the form of a federation, which as such may be revoked on any occasion, and must consequently be renewed from time to time.

This is therefore a right which comes in as an accessory (in subsidium) of another original right, in order to prevent the nations from falling from right and lapsing into the state of actual war with each other. It thus issues in the idea of a foedus amphictyonum.

55. Right of Going to War as related to the
Subjects of the State.

We have then to consider, in the first place, the original right of free states to go to war with each other as being still in a state of nature, but as exercising this right in order to establish some condition of society approaching the juridical And, first of all, the question arises as to what right the state has in relation to its own subjects, to use them in order to make war against other states, to employ their property and even their lives for this purpose, or at least to expose them to hazard and danger; and all this in such a way that it does not depend upon their own personal judgement whether they will march into the field of war or not, but the supreme command of the sovereign claims to settle and dispose of them thus.

This right appears capable of being easily established. It may be grounded upon the right which every one has to do with what is his own as he will. Whatever one has made substantially for himself, he holds as his incontestable property. The following, then, is such a deduction as a mere jurist would put forward.

There are various natural products in a country which, as regards the number and quantity in which they exist, must be considered as specially produced (artefacta) by the work of the state; for the country would not yield them to such extent were it not under the constitution of the state and its regular administrative government, or if the inhabitants were still living in the state of nature. Sheep, cattle, domestic fowl the most useful of their kind- swine, and such like, would either be used up as necessary food or destroyed by beasts of prey in the district in which I live, so that they would entirely disappear, or be found in very scant supplies, were it not for the government securing to the inhabitants their acquisitions and property. This holds likewise of the population itself, as we see in the case of the American deserts; and even were the greatest industry applied in those regions- which is not yet done- there might be but a scanty population. The inhabitants of any country would be but sparsely sown here and there were it not for the protection of government; because without it they could not spread themselves with their households upon a territory which was always in danger of being devastated by enemies or by wild beasts of prey; and further, so great a multitude of men as now live in any one country could not otherwise obtain sufficient means of support. Hence, as it can be said of vegetable growths, such as potatoes, as well as of domesticated animals, that because the abundance in which they are found is a product of human labour, they may be used, destroyed, and consumed by man; so it seems that it may be said of the sovereign, as the supreme power in the state, that he has the right to lead his subjects, as being for the most part productions of his own, to war, as if it were to the chase, and even to march them to the field of battle, as if it were on a pleasure excursion.

This principle of right may be supposed to float dimly before the mind of the monarch, and it certainly holds true at least of the lower animals which may become the property of man. But such a principle will not at all apply to men, especially when viewed as citizens who must be regarded as members of the state, with a share in the legislation, and not merely as means for others but as ends in themselves. As such they must give their free consent, through their representatives, not only to the carrying on of war generally, but to every separate declaration of war; and it is only under this limiting condition that the state has a right to demand their services in undertakings so full of danger.

We would therefore deduce this right rather from the duty of the sovereign to the people than conversely. Under this relation, the people must be regarded as having given their sanction; and, having the right of voting, they may be considered, although thus passive in reference to themselves individually, to be active in so far as they represent the sovereignty itself.

56. Right of Going to War in relation
to Hostile States.

Viewed as in the state of nature, the right of nations to go to war and to carry on hostilities is the legitimate way by which they prosecute their rights by their own power when they regard themselves as injured; and this is done because in that state the method of a juridical process, although the only one proper to settle such disputes, cannot be adopted.

The threatening of war is to be distinguished from the active injury of a first aggression, which again is distinguished from the general outbreak of hostilities. A threat or menace may be given by the active preparation of armaments, upon which a right of prevention (jus praeventionis) is founded on the other side, or merely by the formidable increase of the power of another state (potestas tremenda) by acquisition of territory. Lesion of a less powerful country may be involved merely in the condition of a more powerful neighbour prior to any action at all; and in the state of nature an attack under such circumstances would be warrantable. This international relation is the foundation of the right of equilibrium, or of the "balance of power," among all the states that are in active contiguity to each other.

The right to go to war is constituted by any overt act of injury. This includes any arbitrary retaliation or act of reprisal (retorsio) as a satisfaction taken by one people for an offence committed by another, without any attempt being made to obtain reparation in a peaceful way. Such an act of retaliation would be similar in kind to an outbreak of hostilities without a previous declaration of war. For if there is to be any right at all during the state of war, something analogous to a contract must be assumed, involving acceptance on the side of the declaration on the other, and amounting to the fact that they both will to seek their right in this way.

57. Right during War.

The determination of what constitutes right in war, is the most difficult problem of the right of nations and international law. It is very difficult even to form a conception of such a right, or to think of any law in this lawless state without falling into a contradiction. Inter arma silent leges.* It must then be just the right to carry on war according to such principles as render it always still possible to pass out of that natural condition of the states in their external relations to each other, and to enter into a condition of right.

*["In the midst of arms the laws are silent." Cicero.]

No war of independent states against each other can rightly be a war of punishment (bellum punitivum). For punishment is only in place under the relation of a superior (imperantis) to a subject (subditum); and this is not the relation of the states to one another. Neither can an international war be "a war of extermination" (bellum internicinum), nor even "a war of subjugation" (bellum subjugatorium); for this would issue in the moral extinction of a state by its people being either fused into one mass with the conquering state, or being reduced to slavery. Not that this necessary means of attaining to a condition of peace is itself contradictory to the right of a state; but because the idea of the right of nations includes merely the conception of an antagonism that is in accordance with principles of external freedom, in order that the state may maintain what is properly its own, but not that it may acquire a condition which, from the aggrandizement of its power, might become threatening to other states.

Defensive measures and means of all kinds are allowable to a state that is forced to war, except such as by their use would make the subjects using them unfit to be citizens; for the state would thus make itself unfit to be regarded as a person capable of participating in equal rights in the international relations according to the right of nations. Among these forbidden means are to be reckoned the appointment of subjects to act as spies, or engaging subjects or even strangers to act as assassins, or poisoners (in which class might well be included the so called sharpshooters who lurk in ambush for individuals), or even employing agents to spread false news. In a word, it is forbidden to use any such malignant and perfidious means as would destroy the confidence which would be requisite to establish a lasting peace thereafter.

It is permissible in war to impose exactions and contributions upon a conquered enemy; but it is not legitimate to plunder the people in the way of forcibly depriving individuals of their property. For this would be robbery, seeing it was not the conquered people but the state under whose government they were placed that carried on the war by means of them. All exactions should be raised by regular requisition, and receipts ought to be given for them, in order that when peace is restored the burden imposed on the country or the province may be proportionately borne.

58. Right after War.

The right that follows after war, begins at the moment of the treaty of peace and refers to the consequences of the war. The conqueror lays down the conditions under which he will agree with the conquered power to form the conclusion of peace. Treaties are drawn up; not indeed according to any right that it pertains to him to protect, on account of an alleged lesion by his opponent, but as taking this question upon himself, he bases the right to decide it upon his own power. Hence the conqueror may not demand restitution of the cost of the war; because he would then have to declare the war of his opponent to be unjust. And even although he should adopt such an argument, he is not entitled to apply it; because he would have to declare the war to be punitive, and he would thus in turn inflict an injury. To this right belongs also the exchange of prisoners, which is to be carried out without ransom and without regard to equality of numbers.

Neither the conquered state nor its subjects lose their political liberty by conquest of the country, so as that the former should be degraded to a colony, or the latter to slaves; for otherwise it would have been a penal war, which is contradictory in itself. A colony or a province is constituted by a people which has its own constitution, legislation, and territory, where persons belonging to another state are merely strangers, but which is nevertheless subject to the supreme executive power of another state. This other state is called the mother-country. It is ruled as a daughter, but has at the same time its own form of government, as in a separate parliament under the presidency of a viceroy (civitas hybrida). Such was Athens in relation to different islands; and such is at present (1796) the relation of Great Britain to Ireland.

Still less can slavery be deduced as a rightful institution, from the conquest of a people in war; for this would assume that the war was of a punitive nature. And least of all can a basis be found in war for a hereditary slavery, which is absurd in itself, since guilt cannot be inherited from the criminality of another.

Further, that an amnesty is involved in the conclusion of a treaty of peace is already implied in the very idea of a peace.

59. The Rights of Peace.

The rights of peace are:

1. The right to be in peace when war is in the neighbourhood, or the right of neutrality.

2. The right to have peace secured so that it may continue when it has been concluded, that is, the right of guarantee.

3. The right of the several states to enter into a mutual alliance, so as to defend themselves in common against all external or even internal attacks. This right of federation, however, does not extend to the formation of any league for external aggression or internal aggrandizement.

60. Right as against an Unjust Enemy.

The right of a state against an unjust enemy has no limits, at least in respect of quality as distinguished from quantity or degree. In other words, the injured state may use- not, indeed any means, but yet- all those means that are permissible and in reasonable measure in so far as they are in its power, in order to assert its right to what is its own. But what then is an unjust enemy according to the conceptions of the right of nations, when, as holds generally of the state of nature, every state is judge in its own cause? It is one whose publicly expressed will, whether in word or deed, betrays a maxim which, if it were taken as a universal rule, would make a state of peace among the nations impossible, and would necessarily perpetuate the state of nature. Such is the violation of public treaties, with regard to which it may be assumed that any such violation concerns all nations by threatening their freedom, and that they are thus summoned to unite against such a wrong and to take away the power of committing it. But this does not include the right to partition and appropriate the country, so as to make a state as it were disappear from the earth; for this would be an injustice to the people of that state, who cannot lose their original right to unite into a commonwealth, and to adopt such a new constitution as by its nature would be unfavourable to the inclination for war.

Further, it may be said that the expression "an unjust enemy in the state of nature" is pleonastic; for the state of nature is itself a state of injustice. A just enemy would be one to whom I would do wrong in offering resistance; but such a one would really not be my enemy.

61. Perpetual Peace and a Permanent Congress of Nations.

The natural state of nations as well as of individual men is a state which it is a duty to pass out of, in order to enter into a legal state. Hence, before this transition occurs, all the right of nations and all the external property of states acquirable or maintainable by war are merely provisory; and they can only become peremptory in a universal union of states analogous to that by which a nation becomes a state. It is thus only that a real state of peace could be established. But with the too great extension of such a union of states over vast regions, any government of it, and consequently the protection of its individual members, must at last become impossible; and thus a multitude of such corporations would again bring round a state of war. Hence the perpetual peace, which is the ultimate end of all the right of nations, becomes in fact an impracticable idea. The political principles, however, which aim at such an end, and which enjoin the formation of such unions among the states as may promote a continuous approximation to a perpetual peace, are not impracticable; they are as practicable as this approximation itself, which is a practical problem involving a duty, and founded upon the right of individual men and states.

Such a union of states, in order to maintain peace, may be called a permanent congress of nations; and it is free to every neighbouring state to join in it. A union of this kind, so far at least as regards the formalities of the right of nations in respect of the preservation of peace, was presented in the first half of this century, in the Assembly of the States-General at the Hague. In this Assembly most of the European courts, and even the smallest republics, brought forward their complaints about the hostilities which were carried on by the one against the other. Thus the whole of Europe appeared like a single federated state, accepted as umpire by the several nations in their public differences. But in place of this agreement, the right of nations afterwards survived only in books; it disappeared from the cabinets, or, after force had been already used, it was relegated in the form of theoretical deductions to the obscurity of archives.

By such a congress is here meant only a voluntary combination of different states that would be dissoluble at any time, and not such a union as is embodied in the United States of America, founded upon a political constitution, and therefore indissoluble. It is only by a congress of this kind that the idea of a public right of nations can be established, and that the settlement of their differences by the mode of a civil process, and not by the barbarous means of war, can be realized.

III. The Universal Right of Mankind.
(Jus Cosmopoliticum)
62. Nature and Conditions of Cosmopolitical Right.

The rational idea of a universal, peaceful, if not yet friendly, union of all the nations upon the earth that may come into active relations with each other, is a juridical principle, as distinguished from philanthropic or ethical principles. Nature has enclosed them altogether within definite boundaries, in virtue of the spherical form of their abode as a globus terraqueus; and the possession of the soil upon which an inhabitant of the earth may live can only be regarded as possession of a part of a limited whole and, consequently, as a part to which every one has originally a right. Hence all nations originally hold a community of the soil, but not a juridical community of possession (communio), nor consequently of the use or proprietorship of the soil, but only of a possible physical intercourse (commercium) by means of it. In other words, they are placed in such thoroughgoing relations of each to all the rest that they may claim to enter into intercourse with one another, and they have a right to make an attempt in this direction, while a foreign nation would not be entitled to treat them on this account as enemies. This right, in so far as it relates to a possible union of all nations, in respect of certain laws universally regulating their intercourse with each other, may be called "cosmopolitical right" (jus cosmopoliticum).

It may appear that seas put nations out of all communion with each other. But this is not so; for by means of commerce, seas form the happiest natural provision for their intercourse. And the more there are of neighbouring coastlands, as in the case of the Mediterranean Sea, this intercourse becomes the more animated. And hence communications with such lands, especially where there are settlements upon them connected with the mother countries giving occasion for such communications, bring it about that evil and violence committed in one place of our globe are felt in all. Such possible abuse cannot, however, annul the right of man as a citizen of the world to attempt to enter into communion with all others, and for this purpose to visit all the regions of the earth, although this does not constitute a right of settlement upon the territory of another people (jus incolatus), for which a special contract is required.

But the question is raised as to whether, in the case of newly discovered countries, a people may claim the right to settle (accolatus), and to occupy possessions in the neighbourhood of another people that has already settled in that region; and to do this without their consent.

Such a right is indubitable, if the new settlement takes place at such a distance from the seat of the former that neither would restrict or injure the other in the use of their territory. But in the case of nomadic peoples, or tribes of shepherds and hunters (such as the Hottentots, the Tungusi, and most of the American Indians), whose support is derived from wide desert tracts, such occupation should never take place by force, but only by contract; and any such contract ought never to take advantage of the ignorance of the original dwellers in regard to the cession of their lands. Yet it is commonly alleged that such acts of violent appropriation may be justified as subserving the general good of the world. It appears as if sufficiently justifying grounds were furnished for them, partly by reference to the civilization of barbarous peoples (as by a pretext of this kind even Busching tries to excuse the bloody introduction of the Christian religion into Germany), and partly by founding upon the necessity of purging one's own country from depraved criminals, and the hope of their improvement or that of their posterity, in another continent like New Holland. But all these alleged good purposes cannot wash out the stain of injustice in the means employed to attain them. It may be objected that, had such scrupulousness about making a beginning in founding a legal state with force been always maintained, the whole earth would still have been in a state of lawlessness. But such an objection would as little annul the conditions of right in question as the pretext of the political revolutionaries that, when a constitution has become degenerate, it belongs to the people to transform it by force. This would amount generally to being unjust once and for all, in order thereafter to found justice the more surely, and to make it flourish.

CONCLUSION

If one cannot prove that a thing is, he may try to prove that it is not. And if he succeeds in doing neither (as often occurs), he may still ask whether it is in his interest to accept one or other of the alternatives hypothetically, from the theoretical or the practical point of view. In other words, a hypothesis may be accepted either in order to explain a certain phenomenon (as in astronomy to account for the retrogression and stationariness of the planets), or in order to attain a certain end, which again may be either pragmatic, as belonging merely to the sphere of art, or moral, as involving a purpose which it is a duty to adopt as a maxim of action. Now it is evident that the assumption (suppositio) of the practicability of such an end, though presented merely as a theoretical and problematical judgement, may be regarded as constituting a duty; and hence it is so regarded in this case. For although there may be no positive obligation to believe in such an end, yet even if there were not the least theoretical probability of action being carried out in accordance with it, so long as its impossibility cannot be demonstrated, there still remains a duty incumbent upon us with regard to it.

Now, as a matter of fact, the morally practical reason utters within us its irrevocable veto: There shall be no war. So there ought to be no war, neither between me and you in the condition of nature, nor between us as members of states which, although internally in a condition of law, are still externally in their relation to each other in a condition of lawlessness; for this is not the way by which any one should prosecute his right. Hence the question no longer is as to whether perpetual peace is a real thing or not a real thing, or as to whether we may not be deceiving ourselves when we adopt the former alternative, but we must act on the supposition of its being real. We must work for what may perhaps not be realized, and establish that constitution which yet seems best adapted to bring it about (mayhap republicanism in all states, together and separately). And thus we may put an end to the evil of wars, which have been the chief interest of the internal arrangements of all the states without exception. And although the realization of this purpose may always remain but a pious wish, yet we do certainly not deceive ourselves in adopting the maxim of action that will guide us in working incessantly for it; for it is a duty to do this. To suppose that the moral law within us is itself deceptive, would be sufficient to excite the horrible wish rather to be deprived of all reason than to live under such deception, and even to see oneself, according to such principles, degraded like the lower animals to the level of the mechanical play of nature.

It may be said that the universal and lasting establishment of peace constitutes not merely a part, but the whole final purpose and end of the science of right as viewed within the limits of reason. The state of peace is the only condition of the mine and thine that is secured and guaranteed by laws in the relationship of men living in numbers contiguous to each other, and who are thus combined in a constitution whose rule is derived not from the mere experience of those who have found it the best as a normal guide for others, but which must be taken by the reason a priori from the ideal of a juridical union of men under public laws generally. For all particular examples or instances, being able only to furnish illustration but not proof, are deceptive, and at all events require a metaphysic to establish them by its necessary principles. And this is conceded indirectly even by those who turn metaphysics into ridicule, when they say, as they often do: "The best constitution is that in which not men but laws exercise the power." For what can be more metaphysically sublime in its own way than this very idea of theirs, which according to their own assertion has, notwithstanding, the most objective reality? This may be easily shown by reference to actual instances. And it is this very idea, which alone can be carried out practically, if it is not forced on in a revolutionary and sudden way by violent overthrow of the existing defective constitution; for this would produce for the time the momentary annihilation of the whole juridical state of society. But if the idea is carried forward by gradual reform and in accordance with fixed principles, it may lead by a continuous approximation to the highest political good, and to perpetual peace.

www.ingramcontent.com/pod-product-compliance
Lightning Source LLC
Chambersburg PA
CBHW050812070426

42449CB00045B/400